A Spiritual Rebuild

Volume III

Richard Craig Hughes

DEDICATION

I would like to dedicate this, the seventh book in my compilation of published works, first and foremost to our Lord Jesus Christ, my inspiration. Judging by the lack of enthusiasm of my first volume of memoirs, there may be no more than a dozen readers who finish this book in its entirety. In preparation of that dire statistic, I wrote the original manuscript with the knowledge that Jesus might be the only one who follows my whole story. I wrote it for Him.

CONTENTS

Acknowledgements

1 Introduction   1

2 Prelude   11

3 Young Man on a Mission   40

4 A Fisher of Men   66

5 Forsaken for but a Moment   87

6 The First Rebuild   103

7 Second Rebuild – The Plan   119

8 Disappointment   136

9 Regressing or Digressing?   151

10 Rebuilding with Diesel, and a Revelation   164

11 A Spiritual Rebuild by the Grace of God   217

12 Exercise is of Some Value   292

Epilogue

ACKNOWLEDGEMENTS

I would cordially like to thank everyone who made this book possible, including the Lord God, my wife Kelly, whose unbelievable photographs have often found their way onto the pages of my books, and this one is no exception. The cover shot, by the way, is one she took while we were on vacation in the mountains of North Carolina, a place close to Heaven and both of our hearts. Thanks to all the people whose lives have touched me along the way, whether we worked together, rode together, surfed together, jogged together, competed with or against one another, or studied together in college. And if we played hockey together or I stopped a few of your shots on the net while playing goalie, well I hope I made it challenging for you but not enough to ruin your whole game. Lastly I would like to thank Amazon because I know what it was like to try to get a book published before they made it popular for new authors to publish their own. I have now, with the help of Amazon KDP Select, published seven books in less than five years. The very first manuscript I completed in 1989 still sits on my bookshelf in my home office unpublished, the victim of several rejection slips to various publishing companies. I own the sole copy in existence. So thanks to all of you! I've put a lot into this book and whether the masses read it or not, like the rest of my works, I've put my heart and soul into it.

God Bless,

Richard Craig Hughes

1 INTRODUCTION

As the old saying goes, a lot of water has run under the bridge since the last chapter of Volume I "Memories of a Grateful Soul" happened in real time. Most of you are not familiar with that book but it is a nostalgic look at the past from the early 1960's to the late 1970's, as seen through the eyes of an author born in the Canadian southeast in the late 1950's. That author, the author of this book, and me are one and the same, and I've lived in the American southeast, predominantly Florida, since the age of (almost) eight. I only say predominantly because my wife and I are currently planning to relocate to the mountains of Northeast Georgia someday, perhaps upon my retirement.

To recap, **Volume I** went into pretty fair detail describing what it was like for an (almost) eight-year-old church hockey league-playing-kid from Toronto, Canada to move down to a small town on the east coast of Florida in the mid-1960's. Not trying to plug the first book of this series (much), but it would certainly make my job a lot easier if you the reader were to complete **Volume I** before starting **Volume III**. Then I wouldn't have to explain so much about how a snow-loving Canadian lad made that huge adjustment and transformed into a dirt bike-loving surfboard-toting teenager who loved the beach.

To make that job a little easier I decided to include an excerpt from the epilogue of the precursor to this book, the one that started this whole series, **Canadian Born, American Made,** *Memories of a Grateful Soul* (Amazon, 2017). To wit:

Going back through history, especially one's personal history, with a positive and objective outlook can be a soul cleansing spiritual experience. The irony is, and there is irony in almost everything, once you are old enough to reflect upon at least twenty years of living, many aspects of one's life are beyond the point of no return. You can't go back and change it. But the old adage holds true: Those who do not correct their mistakes are destined to repeat them. So if only to correct mistakes made in the past, recalling one's life history can be helpful toward a better future.

The first twenty years of my life was a time of experimentation. Everything was new, especially after high school graduation. But that was just the tip of the iceberg. I found that at least in my case, the old saying that school days are the best days of one's life isn't always accurate. The first few years **after** *graduation are more than likely the best in terms of discovering one's self and freedom.*

Throughout our lives we meet people who seem to have been born leaders. They just have that self assurance and charismatic air about them. If you have read even a small portion of this book you probably figured out the author was not one of those. I mention several times throughout the manuscript how I looked up to my big brother and how I was so humbled by my best friend John, who was even younger than me.

I feel as if when we begin the journey into adulthood, as many of us do when we come of age, we all begin searching for something. It might be acceptance from our peers or older adults, fame and fortune, the perfect job, the perfect spouse or mate, our purpose in life, or all of the above.

Toward the end of this synopsis of my first twenty years it appears that I had finally found my purpose in life when I learned how to surf. Well that's all well and good as a favorite pastime but it doesn't pay the bills. And one would be hard pressed to find a more enjoyable job than working on a golf course as I did as a young man, but when you are trying to make a living the pay doesn't quite cut it. For the twenty years following 1978, where this book leaves off, I kept searching for better careers. And it only led me to more golf courses and more yard work. Not complaining because I seemed to have a knack for it. The problem was there just wasn't much money to be made in that line of work, so following the next twenty years in 1998 I was still in search of a better career.

The point I am trying to make here, and I know I took the long way around, is that after forty years I still hadn't found what I was looking for. Sound familiar? Aside from being a really good song written by the band U2 back in the 1980's, it is also the plight of dare I say at least 50% of Americans, and we are the people on this planet who have the freedom to do whatever we want in life and go as far as we can dream of going.

So here it is. My life did not change drastically until after I finished reading the Bible and asked God to take over my life. There I said it. Boom. I gave all my decisions to Him. I had no other choice. I just couldn't think of anything I was supposed to do that was in my power and perceived abilities. So I turned it all over to Him and man what a relief! I'm not going to tell you what happened in my life from 1998 through today. That's sure to be another book sometime down the road and it should be a good one. But I will tell you that I did finally become the man that God had intended me to be from the beginning. And now as I am knocking on the door of my sixties I feel closer to Him than I have ever felt in my life, and not because I am better but because I feel like I know Him better. He does actually answer prayer, and my testimony proves it if only in my own eyes. I have witnessed actual miracles in my lifetime and I have witnessed answered prayer. Two things: You've got to have faith and you've got to let God into your life.

In closing let me just say that we are all given choices in this life and there are always forks in the road. When we are young we often have no clue as to which way to turn or which choice to make. We all learn by our mistakes but if I can give you just one heads up in your journey let me give you this advice: It's never too early or never too late to follow God. That's all I am saying.

If you see another twenty-year collection of memoirs by this author somewhere down the road and it skips over a few years just know that it wasn't because I've forgotten huge chunks of my life, but rather because I was working 80-hour weeks between 1992 and 2002 and there's just not that much to write about. But I promise to work on writing down my memories of the magical years when I gave my life over to God and He showed me what His grace and greatness are all about.

Until then be on the lookout for other books I have planned to write…

The "other books" I had planned to write I actually *did* write, and two of them took the place of an official **Volume II** in the *Memories of a Grateful Soul* series. As stated in the Epilogue from **Volume I**, about the only material there was to write about from around the mid-1980's to just after the turn of the 21st century was work, work, and more work. So rather than try to put together another volume of twenty years in my lifetime, I decided to break it down into two books about the careers I specialized in during that time frame. The first one, **Mowing at the Master's Level** (Amazon, 2019), follows my mowing career from the day I first mowed golf course greens on the east coast of Florida in 1977 to my last day mowing fairways on another golf course about five miles away from the first one, as the crow flies, across the Indian River lagoon. Rather than write all about my own exploits, however, I turned the book into somewhat of a manual for readers who want to know if mowing grass could be a career option for them.

The second book, which would have been in **Volume II** if there were such a book, is **Sterile Processing, Invisible Culture** *Reprocessed* (Amazon, 2019), written about the career I have been locked into for thirty years now. It was penned in the same fashion as **Mowing….** as a sort of *guide* for readers who are on the fence as to whether or not they can or should make a career out of sterile processing. I highly recommend this book, as I believe it contains some of my best and most informative writing to date.

If there is any particular theme that every one of my (so far) seven books has in common, it is that they all contain at least a few pages about the virtues of following Jesus Christ as our Savior. Though none of them show any indication from the exterior or subject matter, I included little thoughts and tidbits along the way to show the reader that this author is not going to take credit for any knowledge, wisdom, or accomplishments in life. There isn't enough inside any one of the books to file them under the "Christian" or "Religious" category so no one would have any idea that those tidbits of inspirational text were in there unless they read the entire book.

I decided in the beginning that this book would be different in that respect. I have always wanted to write a Christian book and by golly, this is the one! It probably won't contain enough scripture or Biblical knowledge to please any theologians in the audience, but I have done my best to use the knowledge and wisdom gained in my 62 years, at least half of which I have been a true believer in Christ, to spread the gospel and give my testimony as one whose life was made richer, happier, and more alive with the hope that only faith in our Lord and Savior can provide us as believers.

It has been noted by many Biblical scholars, pastors, and other men and women of the Church that the number seven holds a special place in God's heart. Some have noted that it is mentioned well over seven hundred times in scripture; several times in the Book of Revelation. Some say it translates to "perfection", as it stands for the union of the four corners of the Earth with the Holy Trinity. As I am far from being a Bible scholar I accept the almost unanimous idea that the number seven is truly favored by God the Father of Abraham, Moses, and Jesus. And what is its significance in this book? Only that this is my seventh published manuscript, and it just happens to be my first attempt at writing a Christian book. Call it destiny or coincidence; no one can say for sure. If you think I'm making this up just count every book I have written, published by Amazon, from **Building a Better Goalie Bike** written in 2017, to my sixth book finished last year in 2019, **Sterile Processing, Invisible Culture** and you will see that this is indeed the seventh one. Now I'm not implying that this book was specially chosen by God or that I was chosen to be its author; I wouldn't make such claims because I don't believe the high and mighty statements some of today's evangelists make about how they were chosen to write a particular book, as if it were ordained by God Himself to be read by everybody and make the writer millions. I believe the only book God has chosen for everyone to read is the Holy Bible.

My hope is that He shows favor toward this book and blesses both the words that grace its pages and the people who read them. That is my hope; and may God rain His ample blessings over you and your family.

2 PRELUDE

Sometimes the evidence is right in front of us but we just don't see it. We are always so wrapped up in the moment, the job at hand, or the year ahead of us that we fail to notice the obvious. Yet when we look back a few years, a decade, a quarter century or whenever, there it is staring at us right in the face as if to slap us and say, 'Are you getting any of this?' It is that unmistakable cliché: What comes around goes around. And so I decided for the sake of continuity to start off this chapter based on the golf course I was working on in 1979 because that ten-year career led to a shorter stint on another course twenty years later; the same type of job under much different circumstances.

If you recall from **Volume I** the golfing community where I worked had two courses back then, the North Course and the South Course. In '79 a few of the workers on the North Course were known to 'spark it up' occasionally, or get high. Times were good back then on the golf course. Sometimes when I got caught up with my mowing assignments I would sneak over to the North Course and look for somebody to chat with for a few minutes and then motor on back to the South Course where I belonged. The South Course guys were a little older as a rule and only a couple of guys would get high on occasion. Anyway, I remember cruising around the entire front nine one day on my rough mower and not finding *anybody*. That was pretty weird, I thought. Was everybody working on the back nine? Then, as I was coming up on the 9th green something in my peripheral caught my attention. When I looked over to my right I saw someone at the edge of the woods waving his arms. It was Cliff, another surfer. He was waving at me to bring my machine into the woods from where he came. Well since I was looking for someone anyway, I pulled over to find a little pathway into the woods. Cliff then led the way back to a small clearing in the middle of a thicket. Well lo and behold, there were about four other guys sitting on their machines having a pow-wow in the middle of the woods. I joined them for about five minutes and then headed back to the South Course wearing a big grin on my face. I remember wishing from that point on that I could work on the North Course. But that wouldn't happen for a few more years. Anyway, that's the story of the day I found the North Course crew's favorite hiding spot. I joined their pow-wow a couple more times after that before my supervisor caught me one day as I was coming back onto the South Course. He warned me that if the golf course superintendent ever found out that I was going over to the North Course looking for other workers to chat with I would probably get fired. So that was the end of that. All things must pass.

`John gets a Job at the Golf Course

When the Supper Club closed its doors for good back in the spring of 1977, as you recall from **Volume I**, I took the summer off, went to Toronto on vacation with the family, and then got my first full-time job working on a golf course on the barrier island in Vero Beach. Meanwhile my best friend John had been working on getting his contractor's license and helping his dad maintain his apartments, a part-time job he had held since he was a kid.

By 1979 I guess John was in need of a steady paycheck; either that or he just wanted to work with me again one last time before he began his lifelong career as a builder/contractor. We had worked together for a few months at a famous Fried Chicken restaurant and later on at the Supper Club. Our co-workers and supervisors could always tell we had been friends for a long time. We were like brothers. We wore the same kinds of clothes except I wore sneakers and he wore work boots. We were always cracking each other up with jokes. We rode motorcycles together both on the street and in the woods. We cruised around town in my Malibu and back and forth on 'the strip' by the beach listening to 8-track tapes and combing the area for babes. You name it, we were as close as any brothers you'd ever seen.

So in '79 John got a job at our golf course. He was a hard worker, a common trait among people with a farming heritage. As I said, I don't know why he decided to work there; he was only with us for about 9 months. But the memories we share from those 9 months will last a lifetime. As long as he was working with us on the South Course the North Course crew had nothing on us as far as how much we enjoyed our job. My buddy always had that old-fashioned work ethic; you always work hard for your money but try to enjoy your work too. Let me try to paint a picture here:

I mentioned back in Volume **I** that some of us really enjoyed mowing greens with the hand mowers. Greens mowing machines were designed so that an experienced golf course maintenance worker could mow a green pretty quickly without leaving any marks on the collar, the three-foot wide strip of thicker grass that borders each green. Each worker had their own method but the bottom line was always not to mess up the collar or the machine. And of course the machine had to be running and cutting properly. Most guys, if they wanted to mow super fast, would never shut the throttle down when they made their

180° turn at the end of each pass. My brother actually showed me a method he would use to keep the throttle open the whole time he mowed a green. He would pull his Red Rider cart up to the green and park it, then unload the mower off the back. Most of the time he wouldn't even shut the mower off between greens, but disengage the cutting reel instead so that the blade couldn't inadvertently start spinning while he was driving from green to green. Then when he was ready to start mowing he would find a twig on the ground and jam it in between the throttle lever and carburetor in such a way as to keep the throttle open until he removed the twig after mowing a green. It worked. Anyway, I never used that method; I always liked to have control over the throttle. I just thought it was pretty slick that my brother would come up with something like that. He was always tweaking the machines to his own specs.

So anyway, if I got off the subject a little there, forgive me. I could tell from the first time John mowed greens that he was going to be one of the faster mowers. I would not have expected anything less of him. After he had been working there for a couple of months and knew his way around the golf course, the stage was set for the morning I knew would come. As I mentioned in Book 1, Jack was a middle-aged guy who worked with us on the South Course and loved to mow greens. He said it was a health issue recommended by his doctor but long story short, he voluntarily and willingly mowed the whole putting green every day of the week including weekends, plus the back nine greens on the South Course. So that meant that as a rule our supervisor had only to come up with one other greens mower each morning to mow the front nine greens. Sometimes just to mix things up he would send Jack over to the North Course to mow nine of their greens. I remember one day they let him mow nine greens on the North Course in addition to his beloved back nine greens on the South Course. I believe Jack thought he had finally made it into Heaven that day. He would have probably done that every day had they let him. Anyway when Jack took his vacation in the summer of '79 a few other guys took turns mowing greens for him. John and I were two of them.

Our supervisor pinned the daily work sheet on the board by his office. John was scheduled to mow the back nine greens and I was to mow the front nine. We would split the putting green. The back nine greens were on average a little bigger than the front nine so the front nine mower usually finished before the back nine mower unless he slacked off. The back nine guy kept the front nine guy honest.

We both tried to act like this would be just another morning out on the course mowing greens. John had a way of putting everyone at ease with his sense of humor so we laughed our way over to the equipment barn and picked out our Red Rider carts. I could see that it was going to be business as usual until we got out onto the course and split up, each to our own greens. We cranked up the Red Riders, revved up the engines, and headed over to the gas pump. John filled up his tank then handed me the nozzle and I filled up mine. We headed to the garage where nine greens mowers were neatly parked in three rows of three. John picked the #3 mower. Our head mechanic checked the bedknife on it and gave him the okay. I picked #7, my lucky number. I just hoped it would be fast and sweet for me.

"Hey Pete, is this a good mower?" I asked (the mechanic) while he was still there by the mowers. I figured I would ask him just for good luck. Pete was a busy man, a German born mechanic who did his best to keep our machines running.

"They're all good mowers, Rick," he said with his thick Bavarian accent.

So I loaded up mower #7 with Pete's blessings. Now we were both ready to roll. As John engaged the pulley on his Red Rider with a twist of the left wrist and cranked up the throttle with his right, you could smell the rubber burning from the belt as it spun on the pulley. I followed suit and we both headed out into the dawn. It was the middle of summer and the sun was already coming up on the horizon as we motored our way over to the putting green. The dew lay heavy on the fairways and shone like a light blanket of snow on a chilly Canadian morning in the middle of March. But this wasn't Canada and it sure wasn't snow. It was summertime in Florida and the thermometer was already reading 86° at 7:00 in the morning. Humidity was a balmy 98%. We parked our carts on opposite sides of the green so that our first passes wouldn't mess up the 'striping' effect. After we cranked up our mowers I warmed up the little two-cycle engine for a minute while John took the first pass on the green. His mower was blowing a lot of smoke out of the exhaust but that's pretty normal for a two-stroke until it gets warmed up. After he made his first turnaround I dropped the clutch on my mower and rolled it on over to the green to make my first pass. The heavy dew and healthy growth made certain that visibility would not be an issue. As for racing or trying to finish in a hurry, the biggest issues would be how fast the mowers would go, how well they cut, and how many times we would need to dump our mower buckets on each green. Once we both got underway I tried to gauge whether or not John was already running at full throttle or if he was holding back until he got out onto the course. As for me I had the throttle pinned on the passes but was still shutting down for the turnarounds. Sandbagging? A little perhaps but I didn't want him to think I was actually taking this seriously. I wasn't really. Mowing greens was such a fun job, it involved engines and throttles, and I was finally getting to go head to head with my racing buddy so it was pretty obvious what was going to happen. By the time we were down to our last couple of passes on the putting green both of our mowers were screaming down the greens and barely backing off in the 180° turnarounds. The race was on. With the putting green mowed we still had to set up the 18 miniature pins into the cups before we could take off. John grabbed half and I took half and we hurriedly finished off the job, loaded up the mowers, cranked up the Red Riders, and went our separate ways. As I headed down the dew-covered fairway to the 1st green I looked back over my shoulder as John rode to the 10th green, one of Jack's favorites, to see his mower bouncing around in the cart and his shoulder-length hair (just like mine) streaming out from under his baseball-like cap on this otherwise still Florida morning. I reckoned he was at full throttle. It looked like we had both been blessed with fast machines, so the only advantage in this self-imposed 'race' would be mine because of the overall larger size of the back nine greens. This would be no picnic. But it would be fun.

Mowing greens is the most fun you can have while mowing grass if you like exercising in the great outdoors, especially when the dew is heavy. There is no dust, no bushes or trees to mow around; nothing to worry about except mowing perfectly straight lines and making sure not to knick the collars around the greens. I basically just kept the throttle pinned the whole time that morning and took the smoothest lines from green to green. I'd been mowing these greens at least a couple of days each week for the past two years and was pretty sure I knew the quickest route around the South Course. John on the other hand had been working on the golf course for just a couple of months. It's not rocket science but one would only assume that experience always pays off in the long run. I didn't want to assume anything so I just kept the throttle pinned on that Jacobsen greens mower. The greens were super healthy so I was dumping my grass at least twice on each green; three times on the bigger ones. I wasted no time dumping my basket, figuring that John might even be trying to get by with only dumping once a green. I wasn't sure if that would be a good idea or not. A full basket of grass could slow down a mower substantially, so I stuck with the two baskets- a- green strategy. When I finally made it to the 9th green, directly across the street from the 18th green, John was nowhere in sight. I wondered if he could have gone so fast that he was already done. It was possible I thought, but Holy Toledo he would have had to be *flying*. Plus I should have been able to see him out of the corner of my eye from the 8th green. Perhaps he had come back to the 18th green after mowing the 10th hole and weaved his way back and forth to finish way down the back of the course on the 14th green. Oh well, all I could do was keep mowing. When I was about 1/3rd of the way through the 9th, my last green, John pulled his cart up to the 18th hole. Whew! I could breathe a little easier. But wait; if he had been going fast enough to keep up with me on the back nine I had better keep up the pace because he must have really been hauling the mail. I finished up my last few stripes, made a cleanup pass, yanked my mower up into the Red Rider cart, and shut it down. John was so focused on mowing his last green that I don't even think he realized I was finished. I wrapped the starter rope around the flywheel, brought the 16-horse Briggs & Stratton to life, pulled my cart across the street and parked it by the green. John was on his last few passes. When he caught sight of me he finally broke concentration. He looked a little disappointed but I could tell he had given it his best effort. His shirt was off and was tied around the Red Rider's handlebars. He was covered with grass from head to toe as if he had actually been walking in front of the greens mower where all the freshly cut grass is spewed out from the cutting reel. I don't think I had ever seen anyone get so…. *grassy*, for lack of a better term, from mowing greens. I would find out after a while that John always worked like that. He enjoyed putting 100% effort into everything he did. I sat there waiting for him to finish the green so we could ride into the shop together.

"Man, you must've been hauling ass!" I said after he shut his mower down. He shrugged his shoulders as if to suggest that I still beat him.

"What about you? You finished before me."

"Yeah, but you mowed the back nine."

Then I couldn't help but chuckle at him. I could only imagine him dumping his grass recklessly into his cart. Or maybe he was slinging it behind the greens into the woods. Maybe that was how he ended up wearing half of his cuttings. I waited for him to load up his mower and crank up his cart, then followed him back to the shop. Our first day of greens mower racing was behind us now and John had proven to be a force to be reckoned with. If he were assigned the front nine next time and the tables were turned, how would I fare with the back nine? I'm afraid I don't remember if that day ever came. Jack returned the following week to re-claim the back nine greens and John left the golf course in the fall of that same year. Whatever, it doesn't matter. What mattered then and matters still today is that whatever happens we will always be the best of friends.

Motocross, Surfing, and the Night Life

Ever since the day a surfer friend of mine demonstrated the basic skills and techniques needed for surfing, catching waves became an obsession like nothing I had ever experienced. I wanted to spend every minute of free time out in the water getting better, surfing until the sun went down each day. I envisioned a life of surfing and building surfboards, and wanted to get totally immersed in that lifestyle. Whenever I went to a surf shop to buy surf wax or check out the boards or whatever, I always asked the shop owner or salesperson questions about how their boards were shaped, who shaped them, where did they get their blanks (the foam core of a surfboard), and whatnot. More often than not they would take me to the shaping room to chat with the shapers, who were more than happy to take a break and talk about their work. Most of them were living the life that I had envisioned as the perfect one; surfing and building boards. What could be better? There was just something about it that was so appealing: starting out with a foam blank with squared edges and hand carving it into a shape of one's own unique design, fine sanding it until it was nice and smooth, then fiberglassing and finally the artwork. It was so creative and seemed to fit right in with the surfing lifestyle.

Yes, surfing definitely changed my perception of what happiness was all about, and when John started to get into it we began surfing together after work almost every day. Yet he never really embraced the surfing life; never committed to actually 'being' a surfer but would rather ride his dirt bike. On the other hand, since I had no bike at that time, I just wanted to surf and never really gave dirt bikes a second thought anymore, that is until one day when John, his younger cousin and I were down by the old pier in Vero looking for something to do on a mostly flat ocean in early May. We were jumping off the pier and getting chased back to the beach by a school of stingrays when John brought up the subject of motocross.

"You need to get another bike," he said as we headed back to his old Chevy truck. I just kind of shrugged my shoulders and hadn't thought about bikes since the day I gave up the '77 Honda Elsinore in trade for the '72 Chevy Malibu.

"Ya think?" I said. "I don't know, I haven't really thought about getting back into it."

He said he would be driving down to the Honda shop in a couple of days to pick up some parts for his bike and asked if I would like to tag along.

"Sure," I said. "The waves will probably be flat for awhile anyway."

So we ended up at the Honda shop a couple days later. While John was at the counter picking up his parts I walked over to the showroom to check out the new bikes.

There in the center of the room looking all red and shiny was a brand spanking new CR250R Honda Elsinore. All I could do was marvel at it. The only 250 Elsinore I had ever ridden belonged to a friend of mine who had been out riding at the local dirt bike track while I was out there one day. But that was years ago in 1976 when I still had my '74 Honda CR125. His bike was also a 1974 model so it was really lacking in suspension. But boy did it have the power! The difference in a 250cc and a 125cc racing machine is pretty substantial. A 250 is noticeably bigger, heavier, and faster, and takes a lot more muscle to maneuver it around a rough track, at least in those days. If you were to take a few laps around a track on a 250 then get off the bike and jump on a 125, it would feel almost like riding a toy. The 125 has always had the reputation of being quick handling. Lightning fast reflexes would be a definite plus. The larger the bike the more the rider could rely on extra horsepower to get him out of trouble.

John paid for his parts and walked over to the big red Honda where I was standing. In 1979 this was the biggest bore Honda MX bike on the market. They didn't come out with an open class machine until 1981 and from what I've read about that bike, you wouldn't have wanted one.

"Dude! Nice looking bike!" he said. I could tell he was drooling over it just as badly as I was.

"I'll say. Wonder how much they want for this bad boy."

"Sit on it, man. You know you want to," said John with that knowing smile.

So I grabbed a hold of the handlebars like I owned the thing and sat on it. It just felt right.

"Man that bike is you. How much money did you say you saved up?" asked my buddy. With John standing right there the shop owner wouldn't even need a salesperson on the floor. I had told him not long before then that I had been saving up some money in the bank but didn't know what I was going to do with it. I really had no reason to move out of my dad's house yet as there were only the three of us living there, Dad, my sister and I. Three years out of high school and I still didn't feel like going back to school for anything. So I had all this money in the bank, almost $2000, with no immediate plans on spending it. That's pretty admirable for an almost 21-year-old. Had I kept that frame of mind my entire life I might be sitting on a gold mine by now but that $2000 eventually burnt a huge hole in all of my pockets and it happened right there at the Honda shop when the shop owner finally walked over to us and said,

"Looking for a bike, are you?"

We looked at each other. Then I gave him the old standard,

"No, not really, just lookin'."

"I see. Well if you have any questions you can ask Joel over there. He knows a lot about these machines. If you want to look at any street bikes just let me know," he said and he walked away. The Joel he was referring to was a well known motocross racer who was the sales manager at his shop but was busy with another customer while we were there. I hadn't met Joel before but had heard of him. He was the fastest rider in the area and one of the top riders in the state of Florida, having raced in several national events around the country against riders like Bob and Bill Grossi, Steve Stackable, John Joyner, and Barry Higgins.

"What do you think, man?" asked John.

"It's awesome," I said. "You wanna sit on it?" I asked as I got off the bike and started to put it back on its triangular stand that hooked into the rear axle.

"No, that's alright, I can't afford it," he said.

"Yeah, neither can I, let's go."

On our way home we talked about how awesome the CR250 was and how fast it must have been; about how cool it would be to race it in the 250 class. Forever naïve, we agreed that the 250 class would be a lot easier to trophy in than the 125 class because of how many riders always showed up for the 125 class each week. There had always been at least 40 racers on the starting line at every race we ever entered on our 125cc bikes, and the competition had been fierce. We always felt lucky to finish in the top 10. John looked over at me while he was driving and asked me again,

"So how much money did you say you saved up?"

Another long story shortened up a little, two days later we drove back down to the Honda shop to pick up the bike. I laid out the money on the counter in cash and we rolled the fire-engine red Honda up the ramp and into

John's old Chevy truck for the ride back home. They say a fool and his money are soon parted. I would like to think that there were a lot of worse things I could have done with the $1600. The lessons learned, the pain experienced, the challenges accepted, and the confidence gained earned me wisdom that could not have been achieved simply by going to college. That's what I would like to think. Whether that is the case or not, it contributed to who I became as a young man and who I am today.

Ronald, the guy who sold me my first Honda Elsinore 125, had always said that surfing and motocross went together like football and running track. They complemented each other, both requiring balance and stamina. I agreed with the balance association but never really saw any other similarities, besides them both being individual sports not requiring teammates. Motocross has always taken dedication in the forms of money, time, athletic training, and the element of physical risk. There was a lot at stake every time you lined up behind that starting gate with 30 to 40 other riders bent on finishing the race in the top three. Surfing on the other hand was a sport, a pastime even, that one could enjoy on a peaceful late afternoon with only a handful of other surfers in the water at one's home break. The waves could be big and tough at times but mostly in Florida they glassed off to near perfection during an evening swell.

Combining the two sports felt a little awkward at first, like mixing hockey and soccer: similar goals (ha ha) but entirely different sports. After a while though I thought we had found the recipe for mixing motocross and surfing. We'd load up the bikes on the trailer on Saturday, tie the surfboards to the racks on my Malibu and head for the coast. 'Praying for surf', as all surfers do on a regular basis, we would check out the Sebastian Inlet, Melbourne Beach, and Cocoa Beach and surf until we were all paddled out, then find a motel close to whatever track we were racing on the next day and spend the night. It sure did make for a full weekend. Young and restless, it satisfied our cravings for freedom and adventure, and also gave us a chance to discover different towns and beachside communities in Florida. One thing missing from our racing/surfing weekends that kept us out of trouble was money. We were on a REALLY tight budget, so much so that many times we had just enough for gas, entry fees to the race tracks and cheeseburgers for lunch and dinner.

I'll never forget the weekend we spent the night in Cocoa Beach prior to a Sunday race in Sharpes, a small town just outside of Cocoa. The track, known as Diamondback Cycle Park, or simply 'Diamondback', was one of the toughest tracks in the state of Florida, as witnessed by many amateur, semi-pro, and professional motocross racers of the day. Bob Hannah, Marty Smith, Marty Tripes, Rex Staten, and scores of other professional motocrossers have raced there during the Florida Winter Am series and used it as a training ground to prepare them for the year ahead. Whoop-de-doos deep enough to swallow both bike and rider and sand that turned even the most powerful racing machine into an uncontrollable slippery pogo stick-like experience were the trademarks of Diamondback. So anyway, that's where we were headed on Sunday. Saturday night however, our minds were not on the race but looking for some kind of diversion; the kind that turns many a young man's mind into mush: women! We were looking for some kind of action. So out we went into the night, the first time either one of us had been to Cocoa Beach. We came upon this really cool bar and grill right on the beach on Minutemen Causeway called the 'Anchor Club'. I mean it was really cool, everything I always thought a surfers hangout should look like. We walked in, sat down, had a couple of sodas (John wasn't even old enough to drink yet) and listened to a rock 'n roll band playing some good old songs. It was awesome. We sat there listening to the band for about an hour then decided to check out the bar across the parking lot called the 'Thirsty Turtle'. As soon as we walked into the Thirsty Turtle we knew that this was where we wanted to be. I don't remember much else about the place except that the waitresses were really friendly. There was a guy sitting right behind the door as we walked in asking for a $2.00 'cover charge', which I'd never heard of before. My wallet was looking pretty light but what the heck, we were there to have a good time. There was a girl singing on a stage as we found our seats close to the front so I figured that's why we had to pay the cover charge. If you've never been to Cocoa Beach it's hard to explain the atmosphere, especially the way it was back in the seventies. The bars on the beach were so laid back and rustic, and captured the true spirit of life at the beach. There are still a few of those bars left in Florida.

I'm not even going to pretend to remember what any of the waitresses looked like that evening but suffice to say they must have looked pretty tempting to a couple of young lads from Vero, a town where you don't get too friendly with a girl unless she is your girlfriend. The funny part was we had no idea what kind of bar this was, we just thought there was something *peculiar* about it. A waitress came over after we were seated and asked what we'd like to drink. When John ordered water and I ordered a Coke she laughed and said there was a two drink minimum. Whaaat? I'd never heard of such a thing. First the cover charge and then a two drink minimum? This place wasn't even all that fancy. Then the waitress started dancing right in front of us, a dance that suggested she was flirting and wanted one of us to pick her up; or so I thought. When she looked at me I just shrugged my shoulders to indicate that I had no money.

"Are you *sure* you don't have any money?" she asked as she ran her fingers through my hair.

"Yeah, we don't have any money. We're up here from Vero to go racing tomorrow in Cocoa," I explained.

She smiled and stood up and then walked away. I turned to John and said,

"I guess we'd better leave."

He nodded and we reluctantly walked out the door.

Six o'clock a.m. comes early after a night on the town so we headed back to the motel to get some rest before race day.

Hopes and Dreams of a Young Man

Young adulthood is where it all begins with us. The hopes and dreams we had as kids and adolescents can really take off as we begin to let go of the ties that had bound us to our childhood homes and securities. Yet we must be very careful about the seeds we plant as we go out and "sow our wild oats". For those seeds will affect the rest of our lives, lest we forget the parable in the New Testament about the farmer who sowed seeds in the field with varying results. For those who need a refresher, refer to your Bible in Luke Chapter 8, verses 4 - 15. Because of the nature of God, we know even without reading the whole passage that if a child is raised as a believer in Christ, is Baptized in the faith, and holds onto the Word of God throughout his youth, he can then enter into young adulthood knowing that he or she is living in the Lord's favor. But what of the children and adolescents whose parents or guardians were not Christians; and therefore never got the chance to know or believe in Jesus Christ? Will they be forsaken by God while they are here on Earth and later on in His Kingdom?

It's pretty obvious from what you have read so far in the *Prelude* that the author was not one of those children in whom the Word was planted early in life and took root. My parents were both good people, having been raised in the "greatest generation", tempered by wars, depressions, recessions, and other adversities, having survived and raised three kids into adulthood. Yet my Dad was either never really a believer or he had lost his faith somewhere along the way; we never got around to talking about it. So this is the premise on which the beginning of my story, my journey into adulthood, begins; as a young man seeking the answer to all of life's difficult questions, looking for that pot of gold at the end of the rainbow, not knowing what a pot of gold looks like or even who to ask. Stick with me if you think you have the patience, because it was a **long long** journey until I finally found out the hard way that you never find your pot of gold unless Jesus Himself shows it to you and it will both satisfy you beyond your wildest dreams and also bring glory to His Father, God Himself. Amen to that!

3 YOUNG MAN ON A MISSION

Okay so this is the chapter that you readers who have no interest at all in motocross racing should probably just skip. 1980 was my all-out assault on the Florida amateur motocross racing circuit. Nothing else even mattered that year. It was the closest I ever came to being a genuine motocrosser in my life. My racing partner that year eventually called it "The year that was." If it weren't for Chuck and his family this whole chapter would almost certainly not exist, at least not as a full season of competitive Florida motocross racing. A little background here:

Chuck started working as an irrigation specialist on our golf course in late 1979. He was so aloof with such an inconspicuous nature that I hadn't even known he was working with us until he approached me one day and introduced himself. He had heard that I raced dirt bikes and had coincidentally just bought a brand new 1979 Honda CR250. I thought that was a little strange from the get go. But he was friendly and persistent and seemed to want my friendship as well. Having grown up in a small town however, and not that outgoing, I was not one to try to make new friends, especially if they were from out of town. Chuck's family had just moved down from Georgia. Apparently he and his younger brother had done quite a bit of racing up there. Eventually his persistence did pay off and we began running together to train our legs and lungs for motocross. Chuck trained with weights too but I never really got into the weight training regimen. Looking back I wish I had. Weight training is, as one of my high school teachers used to say, a great 'equalizer.' I had been running the beach for some time but Chuck had discovered a new trail down by the river called Riverside Park. It was a beautiful trail almost exactly a mile in length that wound around large oaks, tennis courts, workout stations, and the city boat docks. It had an almost perfect consistency of shells, dirt, and sand and was soft enough that it never caused any joint pain that I can recall. I had considered myself a miler until I started running with Chuck. My best time for the mile was 5:25, recorded by my sister at our high school track in 1976 shortly after I graduated. But Chuck had been running five times around the Riverside track since he moved to Vero with a pace of about 6:30 per lap/ mile. The first time we ran together around Riverside it was such an easy pace that we both could talk rather easily while we ran. But whenever we got to the fifth and last lap I could tell he would always speed up. A runner just knows. Down the back stretch by the river with about 1/8th of a mile left, Chuck would open it up. And he did that every single time we ran that trail together. It became somewhat of a game after awhile. I would try to out guess him as to when he would start his sprint. I once tried to break into a sprint with a ½ mile to go, only to burn out a ¼ mile later. I even tried to mentally slow him down on the last lap to save energy in the hopes of beating him down the stretch. But no matter what strategy I tried Chuck NEVER let me beat him to the finish line down by the river's edge. We had races so close that he would make sure he touched the pole first at the end of the trail just so I knew that he had beaten me once again. But I never once got mad at him for beating me. We had become friends. He wasn't a humble person by any stretch; he took pleasure in reminding me that he had beaten me in every single race. (I did beat him once, but that's another story; wait for it.) But it was the way he tried to help me get faster and become a better and stronger person that showed me Chuck had a good heart.

I finally got to race Chuck for real one weekend when he showed up at Diamondback in Cocoa with his new Honda CR250. An old neighbor of mine Dave, who grew up with the 28th Avenue gang, tagged along with me to watch some good old Florida motocross. He would later buy his own Suzuki RM250 and go racing with us but that's another story. Anyway once we got to the track and unloaded the bikes Dave and I started walking around the pits checking out other bikes. He and I had been arch rivals on our neighborhood track when we were kids, he on his 1973 Suzuki TS90 Honcho and me on my 1971 Kawasaki 90 Bushmaster. After weaving our way through all the bikes, riders, and families in the pit area, Dave and I finally made it to the starting area, where practice was just about to begin. The mini-bikes would be first, followed by 125's, 250's, and on and on, just like the regular racing program order. There were several other riders standing by the starting line watching how the gate was falling on that particular day and where the best line would be to the first turn. One rider I noticed was standing alone with his arms folded staring out at the first turn intently. Tall and lanky and facing the other way, he had kind of an old-fashioned haircut that stood out among most of the rest of us with longer hair. I remember he was wearing jeans that were pulled up to his waist like what we used to call 'high-waters.' In no way, shape or form did this guy look like a racer. Rather he looked more like a big goofball. When he turned his head I realized it was Chuck. We would be racing in the same class that day.

'This should be fun,' I thought.

When the announcer called for the 250 Novice class to go to the staging area later that morning I made final preparations on the bike and donned my shoulder pads, helmet, goggles, and gloves. Like most of the riders I preferred to put my riding pants and boots on after the riders' meeting and leave them on until after the second moto. I cranked up the CR250 on the second kick and warmed it up a little before heading over to the starting gate. Thoughts of dueling it out with Chuck began flashing through my mind as I rode down the grassy trail, and I immediately dismissed them.

'Nah,' I thought. *'I probably won't even see him the whole moto.'*

When I got to the starting line Chuck was already there. He grabbed an inside spot on the gate, one that would take him to the inside of the first turn. Now I was certain he didn't know what he was doing. Everyone I knew had always recommended outside lines at Diamondback, from the starting line to the finish line. It was a rough track, one of the roughest in Florida, and Florida has always been known for its rough sandy tracks. The turns there were wide and bumpy with berms that would get so thick you could just lay your bike over and turn the throttle wide open with no worries about sliding out or high-siding. You did have to worry about slamming into the bumps so hard they would throw you over the bars. The theory was that if you held the gas on everywhere you could take all the outside lines and take every turn a gear higher than the guy who had to brake to dive to the inside of the turns. At least 85% of the time the theory worked. A rider who had the throttle pinned taking outside lines all the way around the track could count on beating 85% of the pack. If he pulled the holeshot chances are nobody would ever catch him. But there are always a handful of riders in any given race who actually *study* the layout of a racetrack in order to find the quickest lines around the entire track. In other words they try to seek out the big picture, looking at the overall fastest line around the whole track instead of just nailing all the berms. And there lies the rub: the thinking rider versus the fearless, wild and crazy rider. There are thinking rider race tracks and there are crazy rider tracks. If I had to guess I would say that Diamondback was more of a crazy rider's track. The sand and the whoops were so deep and the turns so thick they just begged for a wide open throttle. But they didn't call it Diamondback because of the rattlesnakes in the area, although there may have been a few in the woods. That track wound and twisted its way from the first turn through the last turn by the grandstand and the checkered flag. And when you've got a winding and twisting track about 15 to 20 feet wide all the way around, you've got an opportunity to shorten your lines by knowing the quickest way around it. I will illustrate this theory in more depth a little further into the chapter.

I rode my bike across the starting chute past Chuck, gave him a wave and a nod, and lined up closer to the outside line to the first turn. I was hoping to show him that the outside line was the best one at this track and maybe help him out a little. Instead I was right. I did not see Chuck the whole moto. I had gotten off to a mediocre start, about mid-pack, and lost sight of him, almost certain he had been behind me for the entire race. But after the moto it was the strangest thing. I rode past his pit area on the way back to mine and there he was, already sitting in his mom's car with the door open and a towel around his neck eating a sandwich. At that point I was sure he DNF'd (did not finish the race). I waved to him like I had before the race, he gave me a big grin and a thumbs up, and I rode back to my pit area. As I lifted my bike up onto its milk crate stand, Dave was just getting back from the tunnel jump, where he had watched almost the entire race.

"Nice ride Rick," he said.

"Thanks man."

"Hey your friend Chuck won the race."

I looked at Dave in total amazement, not sure if he was joking or serious.

"WHAT?"

"Yup. Pulled the holeshot and he was gone. Nobody really challenged him. He didn't look like he was going all that fast but nobody could catch him. He's not all that smooth either."

I let that sink in for a minute; how I was so sure he was behind me from the start; how I thought he looked too goofy to be fast; and how I had totally misjudged and underestimated his capabilities just because he didn't fit the stereotype I had for a fast motocrosser. And all I could think about was how ignorant and stupid I felt at that moment. I had truly been humbled once again by this 19 year-old who had befriended me at work only a couple of months earlier. Why would I have thought that I was so much faster than him just because of his haircut and the way he wore his jeans? That was a real eye opener. I don't know how much it affected the rest of my life as a whole but I do know that I would never ever judge a rider by anything less than the way he rode a motorcycle from that day on.

Chuck ended up winning the second moto as well. After the race he walked by my pit area carrying the huge 1st place trophy, and holding it up for me to see.

"Hey Hughes!" he said with that goofy grin of his.

"Wow, way to go man!" was all I could think of to say. Naturally I was jealous. What racer could deny it? We were all after that 1st place trophy, especially at Diamondback. Their trophies were huge. His was probably about three feet tall with two columns, one on each side, that ran a third of the length up from the bottom; a real beauty.

Like I said I was humbled. And I didn't even know back then that God wants us to be humble at all times. So it just made me feel inferior instead of feeling right with the Lord. I know now that if winning is your goal and you pursue it with all your heart and humble yourself before the Lord, showing patience, mercy, and kindness; it is only a matter of time before victory is yours. But you must give the victory to Him who gave you the victory. God wants the glory; after all it is His to claim. You are just an instrument. Believe me or don't, but that is the surest way to victory.

The 1980 Winter AMA Series

The Florida Winter Ams became an annual event in 1970, touted by the AMA (American Motorcyclist Association) as a great way for the pros and semi-pros to get in shape for the upcoming season. Naturally there was a lot of truth to this but the bottom line for the AMA was that it brought the American pros down to Florida for the winter. Brad Lackey, Jimmy Weinert, John DeSoto, and almost the entire Team Kawasaki came down in 1973. When Bob Hannah first rode the Florida series in the winter of 1976 it was literally 'Bob who?' After he won every single race in his class and then went on to destroy Marty Smith's reputation as the fastest rider in the 125cc class that same year, his name soon changed to 'Hurricane Hannah.' Twenty years later another legend was coming of age in the deep sandy whoops of Florida. Clearwater, Florida native Ricky Carmichael has since set many records in both supercross and outdoor nationals that will probably never be broken, including two perfect seasons in the U.S. national series, in which he won all 24 motos in each of the two years 2002 and 2004.

In the winter of 1980 my friend Chuck wanted to run the amateur portion of the Winter AMA series. The amateurs ran on Saturday, the day before the pros. And he didn't want to go to the races by himself so he talked me into racing the series with him. Now I was just getting used to my Honda 250 at that time and was still no threat to any of the top riders in the Novice class. Plus my bike was still bone stock. The first order of business, according to Chuck, was to buy a set of Fox air shocks. That would at least put me closer to the ballpark of what the other riders were running. The Honda motor would run with most anything out there short of a professionally tuned racing machine, but the chassis was not up to par with the Suzukis, the Yamahas, and of course the

Maicos. Only Kawasaki had perhaps a more inferior handling bike than the 1979 Elsinore 250. So the goal was to make the bike more competitive in order to have at least a fighting chance in the series. In the spirit of my generation I decided to 'go for it'; bought a brand new pair of leathers, two new knobbies for the front and rear, a Bell Moto III full face helmet and the recommended pair of Fox air shocks. With all that new equipment I even *looked* like a serious racer instead of a rookie. I was ready to take on the challenge of the Florida Winter Series, or so I thought.

The Series opener was in St. Petersburg on the west coast of Florida, a track I'd never ridden in my life. The texture was more of a clay than the deep sugar sand I was used to from racing Diamondback, the Orlando Sports Stadium, and Orange County Raceway in Bithlo; much more hard-packed. The jumps were nothing spectacular. There was a really steep one about twenty feet high called McCoy's Mountain, made famous by Florida's own local hotshoe Monte McCoy, who I imagine used to turn it into a sky shot. But it was definitely doable. And speaking of hotshoes they were all there that day. Every rider in the state of Florida and many from around the country who considered themselves fast enough to compete with Florida's best were there to line up on that starting gate and give it their all. Practice was a zoo. There must have been well over a hundred riders out there bouncing around trying to get a feel for the track and its turns, jumps, straightaways, whoop-de-doos, and other features. Problem was we spent much more time trying to avoid the riders that were either riding up our rear wheels or crashing in front of us. It was crazy. After practice Chuck told me that the track would be rough by the time our race came around. And he meant *really* rough. When Chuck said a track was rough you could count on bouncing around like a pogo stick. He loved rough tracks. He lived for rough tracks, modeling his training program after pros like Bob Hannah and Roger DeCoster, who preyed on weaker riders who couldn't hang with them when the whoops grew so deep they would swallow up both bike and rider and spit them out over the top of the next rut.

And Chuck was right. I thought I had ridden rough tracks before, having raced Diamondback and the

Orlando Sports Stadium on several occasions. But this was different. Since there were so many riders in each class they had to have qualifiers for each race, which meant 45 riders would have to go out at a time and try to qualify for their heat, the top 15 riders advancing from each qualifier to the actual motos. I approached the start somewhat cautiously; after all I realized that most of the other riders on the track were on a totally different level. My objective was to make it through the first turn and then just try to qualify. When the starter held up the 15 second sign the sound of 45 riders winding out their machines to 'clean' them out was enough to get the adrenaline flowing if it wasn't already. When the gate dropped, that sound turned into a deafening roar like that of an airplane turning up the throttle in its hangar. As expected the really fast guys fought over the first turn and the rest of us just tried to get through it without incident, a feat in itself. The race to me just felt like an extension of the practice zoo. The track was so bumpy that you couldn't actually open the bike up anywhere to utilize the power of the bike's motor to try to pick up a few places in the pack. It was a bit depressing; I mean I was enjoying the fact that I was out there with probably the best riders in the Southeast but it was all too obvious that I didn't belong there though it certainly was good training, that much was for sure. I couldn't pass anyone and it got to be pretty aggravating after a couple of laps. After the race even Chuck seemed disappointed with my performance and that's what hurt my pride the most I suppose.

"Why didn't you pass anyone?" he asked.

"I don't know, most of the time I was just trying to keep it up on two wheels," I said. We were both obviously disappointed with my race.

"That's no way to race, Hughes. You've got to go for it, man! Next week you've got to start passing people or you're never going to qualify for any of the races in the series. Come on, man!"

Chuck was right. He qualified for his moto. So I spent the rest of the afternoon watching him race. Dave had been right too. Chuck had a unique style. He didn't look fast but he kept picking off other riders each lap. He didn't look smooth over the bumps. You couldn't say he took the best lines. To be honest sometimes it looked like he was taking the roughest lines around the track. But it *worked* for him because he relished the fact that he was one of the toughest riders out there. That was his credo and he stuck with it. Whenever he crashed the bike he was half disappointed and half proud of it. I had never known anyone like that before so it was a little strange before I got used to it. My old racing buddy John, whom I had ridden with almost exclusively since 1974, had always seemed like a pretty tough rider to me. I once watched him not only finish a race but trophy after his footpeg broke off on the second lap at the Orlando Sports Stadium in 1976. And that was on his '74 Elsinore with the old standard shock placement, racing against riders on brand new bikes with forward-mounted Fox air shocks, air forks, the works. John was no easy rider. But this was different. I had never known anyone before Chuck who would gloat about breaking his frame during a race or about finishing a race with a flat front tire; or crashing on the first lap, getting back up and passing ten riders before crashing again. No, Chuck was different from anyone I had ever hung around with. I once watched him come in from a mud race with his eyes almost totally sealed shut with mud. I don't even know how he could see. I wasn't so sure I wanted him as my new racing partner but he seemed to want me as his.

So after a disappointing race for both of us at the opener in St. Pete (Chuck had crashed too many times to be in contention), we went through the usual motions at the golf course during the week, training every other day in the process, and then headed up to Orlando for the second race of the series.

Orlando Sports Stadium
February, 1980

The distinct smell of two-cycle oil burning hung in the morning air like bacon in the kitchen of a Cracker Barrel. When we pulled my Malibu into the pits of the Sports Stadium several riders had already unloaded their bikes and were either prepping them for the day's races or 'cleaning them out' on the practice section next to the main track. A quick look around before we found a place to park suggested what I had tried to prepare myself for all week long; there would be even more serious racers here in Orlando than there had been in St. Pete on the previous weekend. The Sports Stadium had a reputation back then as sort of a hub in Central Florida where all the fast riders could test their skills against each other. Seeing all the new bikes sitting on their stands with all the state-of-the-art technology and knowing that the pilots could ride those bikes to their full potential was more than slightly intimidating. It was downright nerve racking. We wasted no time in finding a decent place to pit. If Chuck was nervous he never let it show, although I did notice that he was really focused and deep in concentration once we motored into the pits. I faintly remember some of the conversations we used to have about big races such as this one. He would ask me if I was nervous and when I admitted that I was he would assure me that there was nothing to be nervous about.

"Those guys might look intimidating, but just remember that you train just as hard as or harder than they do, don't you?"

Of course I couldn't argue with him. After all, we trained together and I knew he trained hard so he was right. For a 19 year-old he was mature way beyond his years, to be able to calm a buddy's nerves like that two years his senior.

"Just go out there and try to pass as many riders as you can. Hold the throttle on longer into the turns and you can pick off riders every lap."

That was another great piece of advice that always sounded easier in theory than in actual racing conditions; reason being that any rider worth his salt knew that trick. Every challenge of seeing who could hold the throttle on the longest into a turn or over a jump turned into a balls-to-the-wall race into each turn with each rider brake checking the other. But that's racing. The only way I could truly look at the races in the Winter Am series was as a great opportunity to race with a LOT of fast riders over the toughest tracks in the state of Florida. In other words the experience alone would make it all worthwhile.

So I suited up for practice and headed over to the starting area while the 125's rode their last few laps of practice. As I sat on my bike waiting for the inevitable moment to arrive when all the 250's would be unleashed onto the track, another rider pulled up next to me on a

Yamaha YZ 250. When I looked at the back of his jersey I couldn't believe it. It was Steve Martin; no, not the famous comedian but rather the super fast Florida pro national rider who would later move to Japan to become a two-time Japanese national motocross champion. And there he was lined up *beside me* for practice. That really put things into perspective. The big boys were definitely there and I would get to ride with them, even if it was only in practice.

When the last 125 rider crossed the finish line the starter/referee began waving us onto the race track in groups of ten riders at a time at ten-second intervals. Steve Martin went out in the group before mine. By the time we took off he had already roosted around the first turn and was shifting gears down horsepower straightaway toward the tabletop jump. The starter waved us on and my group got underway. Much like St. Pete the weekend before, we were only the third class of riders to hit the track, after the mini-bikes and 125's, and the track was already rougher than it normally would be by the end of the day on a regular racing weekend. Orlando was a sand track; not the deep power-robbing sand of a track like Diamondback, but sand easily molded by the hoards of dirt bikes braking into turns and bouncing over jumps and whoop-de-doos lap after lap after lap. And hot. Orlando has never been blessed by the sea breezes coming off either the Gulf or Atlantic coasts. Instead the summer heat just seemed to hover over the central part of the state as if the sun itself were a million miles closer than in anywhere else in the world.

Regardless, I made it around the first lap and felt a little more confident than the week before in St. Pete. Perhaps I would qualify. Dust didn't seem to be a problem, only the severity of the ruts that kept worsening with each lap of practice. Smaller speed bumps that were a mere hazard on a regular Sunday were fast becoming downright ledges before the racing program even began. But midway through our second lap of practice a much bigger problem soon presented itself. As I exited the right-hander before the tunnel jump about 50 yards away a rider was slowing down as he headed towards the jump. With riders on either side of me I was forced to take the same line as the slowing rider. When he got to the jump, so big there was a pedestrian tunnel underneath it, he suddenly stopped halfway to the top. At a loss as to how I was supposed to react to this stupidity I did something even more stupid. I stopped right behind him. What else was I supposed to do? Well apparently the right thing to do whenever a rider stops in front of you on the track during the Florida Winter Series was to run him over, which is exactly what happened to me instead. As I put my left foot down to keep from falling over, the next rider behind me ran over my leg doing about 50 mph. I fell to the ground and instinctively rolled off the track, leaving my bike lying on the front side of the jump. Kid you not, the rider who felt compelled to stop in the middle of the jump just seconds before miraculously was able to get his bike going again and rode off. Meanwhile I tried to get up and run over to pick my bike up off the track, but my left leg was not cooperating. It collapsed under my weight and I fell right back onto the ground. I knew my leg was broken. It didn't hurt, probably because it was such a clean break; but I could not support any weight on it. I lay back down on the side of the track waiting helplessly for practice to end so that someone could hopefully help me back to the pits. Instead the ambulance weaved its way over to where I was lying and the medics came out to ask me what had happened. I just told them what I knew at the time, that my leg was broken. They took my word for it and left my boots on until I got to the hospital where they cut my left one off so as not to disturb the fracture. I must have waited in the ER at the hospital in Orlando for at least two hours before they finally got a doctor to check me out. When he got there I overheard him ask the ER team what the problem was.

"What do we have here?" he asked, just like they did on TV, while looking at my chart.

"We've got a guy that's been lying here waiting patiently for the past few hours with a badly broken ankle," was the answer.

He approached me, introduced himself and told me that he and his team would take good care of me.

"I hear you've been waiting quite some time. You've got a badly broken ankle but we're going to take care of it for you. We'll get you into surgery, put a couple of screws in there and maybe some plates, you'll most likely spend a night or two in the hospital and then we'll let you go. You'll have to check back with us in a week or so of course so we can monitor your progress and take it one step at a time. I can't promise you your ankle will ever be as strong as it used to be but we will do our best. Okay?"

"Yes sir. Thank you," I said, relieved that a doctor finally showed up.

So they operated, put screws in my tibia and fibular bones to hold them together, and hoped for the best. The doctor later told me when he cut the last of three different casts off that I would probably never get full strength back into my left ankle joint and that I would probably never walk without a limp, just because of how completely the bones had been snapped in two just above the ankle joint. I suppose in a way he was right. It took several years, perhaps over a decade, before I lost most of my limp, as my left ankle just didn't seem to have the strength to flex while walking. But I have been a greens mower, a lawn maintenance worker, and a runner as well, and have walked and run God only knows how many thousands of miles in my lifetime. And I can tell you that following my running career my right ankle gives me more problems than my 'bad' left ankle does nowadays, to the extent that it is my right ankle that has been keeping me from doing any running since my last race in May of 2016.

So a big 'thank you' to that Orlando doctor for building me a strong enough ankle out of two completely broken bones to propel me through the end of my motocross racing career, the prime of my running career, 25 more years of surfing, and a hockey career that continues to this day.

4 A FISHER OF MEN

Unless or until a young man or woman has figured out their pathway to success, there is always that uncertainty about what the future will bring. There are so many choices, so many directions from which to choose. They were abundant when I was young; even more so in today's hyper-technological society. If I had to guess I would say that the top two choices most American parents have always hoped and prayed their children would pick from would be between going to college and joining the armed forces. Both of those options have a pretty good track record of eventually leading to good civilian jobs/ careers.

Like most parents, my dad sat me down at a young age, around 16 I think, and told me it was time to start thinking about what I wanted to do for work after high school. Perhaps I had never given it much thought because I told him all I wanted to do was race motocross. That didn't sit too well with Dad. For whatever reason, he *never* liked motorcycles, and he *for sure* didn't want either of his sons racing them for a living. So he came up with all kinds of reasons why racing motocross would be a poor career choice. They were all good reasons, you know the usual: injuries, not enough money, only the top riders in the country can make a living (very true in the 1970's), and a couple other good ones. But that's what I wanted to be back then. In reality, I just couldn't think of any real job that would interest me enough to warrant going back to school. Fast-forward forty years and I still haven't landed what anyone would consider a dream job. Guess it was never in the cards.

So after 1980, 'the year that was' as Chuck called it, the feeling of uncertainty came back and began to really fester in my frontal cortex, the part of the brain that controls "thoughts and actions in accordance with internal goals", according to Wikipedia. Those kinds of feelings are uncomfortable enough for middle-aged people and beyond. For teens and young adults, they can make one sick in the stomach and feel emotionally unstable at the very least.

When Dad once again sat me down after the 1980 racing season, in which I finished a respectable 2nd place overall in my class, he asked what was next. Without hesitating I replied that I wanted to win my class the next season, in 1981. He seemed okay with it, which really shocked me because I wasn't even totally okay with it myself. The irony was, all the reasons he had rattled off before about the dangers and high costs of racing had been true, and I had experienced them both during the past racing season. Having had no health insurance to pay for all the doctor bills resulting from a broken ankle suffered at the Orlando Sports Stadium, I was already in so much debt it would take years to pay off. And that resulted in only a 2nd place finish in the series. What kind of sacrifices would be required in the pursuit of victory in the series the following year? These things really began to weigh heavily on my frontal cortex. What was a young man to do?

Well one thing I began to do more frequently was to go back to one of my all-time favorite passions: surfing. There is just something about it that takes any kind and amount of stress and throws it out the front window of the cortex, if you will. (See what I did there?)

Fall gives way to winter and the ocean becomes increasingly less inviting. Even a wetsuit isn't much comfort to a Floridian when water temperatures are in the sixties and the wind-chill factor is hovering in the forties. The less dedicated surfers prefer to stay home and dry on those dull and dreary, windy wintry days.

The air temperature was around 45 degrees with a northeast wind blowing at 20 to 30 miles per hour. Water temperature was a nippy 62 degrees. The beaches were empty.

On that chilly Saturday morning there were about a dozen surfers out at the local beach; die-hards. Forget the winds and temperatures. These guys only comprehend wave size. On that day the waves were unusually big, a wind-blown 8-10 feet. They weren't breaking clean but Florida waves are nothing like Hawaiian waves, not even Caribbean waves.

I sat in the warmth of my Malibu in the parking lot watching those guys go for the cold and nasty grinders that were breaking about fifty yards or so off the beach. Rock 'n roll was playing on the tape deck as I contemplated whether or not to join them when who pulled up beside the car but Mike, a semi-pro Florida surfer, in a piece of junk pickup truck that would have been hard-pressed to last 10 more miles.

Mike rolled down his window.

"Goin' out, brother?" he said, leaving his truck struggling to idle while he checked out the surf conditions. An occasional rev of the engine kept it from dying out completely.

"Don't know yet. Got all day. It might settle down after awhile," I replied, not quite ready to leave the warmth of my car for the wintry conditions outside yet.

"Man, this break is lame anyway. Want to go to the Inlet? I'll give you a couple dollars for gas."

I chuckled to myself and thought,

'At least this guy doesn't think that piece of junk would make it all the way to the Inlet.'

"Yeah, sure, let's go." I said, and we threw his board on the rack on top of the Malibu.

About four miles down the road, halfway to the Inlet, I began to wonder how big the waves might be, knowing that Mike would more than likely surf any wave in Florida under any condition. Professional surfers are hard core. To them the element of fear must remain in the far reaches of their minds, back there with the thought of a 40-hour work week.

A panic-stricken surfer facing 10 – 15 foot swells might just as well be surrounded by sharks of the same size.

"Could be big," said Mike.

'Yeah, but *how* big,' I wondered. Not wanting to look like a gremmie, I kept my thoughts from Mike and tried to show no fear. But raw guts cannot be staged. And every man has to draw his own line.

"Well if it's really big I'm not going out," I said.

"Yeah right," said Mike.

Mike had drawn the line. If I didn't go out, I would be a non-surfer for sure.

Not a word was spoken until we reached the top of the bridge directly over the inlet. The jetty was in plain sight.

"Yeah it's big. We're going to have to jump off the jetty. The current's too strong to paddle out," said Mike matter-of-factly.

"I'm not going out," I said, still looking straight ahead and not wanting to look over at Mike who could already taste his first wave. Then, being young and restless myself I just shrugged and said, "Oh well, what the heck. Let's park this thing. Think we can squeeze in somewhere?" The parking lot was empty except for four other surfers' cars and about seven or eight fishermen's cars. The waves would surely be massive, or else the place would have been packed.

"I'm not a real strong swimmer, Mike. I'm not too sure about this, you know?"

"Just follow me."

After donning wetsuits Mike led the way from the parking lot down to the jetty. As we made our way over the dune line the waves suddenly came into view. Mike saw them first.

"Alright! A solid eight to ten!"

"Holy crap!" was about all I could add. What a **real** surfer calls *eight to ten feet* looks more like two stories to the average Joe.

By now Mike had sensed my uneasiness over the size of the swell. But he couldn't really know how inexperienced I was in large wind-blown surf. After all, I was 22 years old. At 27 Mike had over 15 years of experience as a surfer. To him a 10-foot Florida wave was just about the right size to shred on. Concerned about the treacherous storm currents? That was doubtful. Mike's favorite break was the Inlet. When the waves jumped up to the 10 to 15-foot range there would only be about five to ten men out there surfing and Mike would be one of them. You could bet on it.

On the other hand, I had been mostly into motocross as a teenager. I knew every professional racer's name, both American and European, rode my bike every chance I got, and went through almost a dozen dirt bikes before all but abandoning that sport for surfing. With only three full years of surfing behind me, I would be a fool to attempt a big day at the Inlet.

But the thought of gaining more respect from Mike, or at least not losing any, kept me from backing out of what would soon become a desperate situation.

"Doesn't look like 10 foot to me," I said, trying to act brave.

"Wait till you get out there. Don't worry, it gets bigger," said Mike. "All that foam makes it look smaller from here."

"Yeah, how do we get past all of that white water anyway?"

"When they're this big you don't paddle out. We're going to jump off the jetty, like I said. It's easy," Mike said as we made our way through the empty parking lot and headed down the long boardwalk that meandered its way to the jetty.

The jetty was a concrete slab about a hundred yards long and ten feet wide, supported by massive concrete girders about seven feet apart. It stood about ten feet over a bed of huge boulders covered with algae and barnacles. It was a beautiful structure; a Florida landmark.

As we stepped onto that beautiful Florida landmark we could see what we were dealing with. Waves were breaking all along the jetty, anywhere from fifty to about a hundred yards out. Good footing was essential, as the concrete was a mixture of fish guts and salt water. It was time for Mike to take control.

"We're going to walk almost all the way to the end, past the first break. If you don't go far enough out the white water will get you. And you don't want to be thrown against those rocks."

Walking towards the end of the jetty, waves crashing on either side, we passed a few fishermen. I couldn't help but wish I were one of them at that moment, instead of being a crazy surfer jumping into what would surely be oblivion. Mike continued,

"Okay we're past the break. What you want to do is step over the rail, stand just on the other side of it, hold your board under your shoulder like this, and jump. As soon as you hit the water get on your board and start paddling as hard as you can. Got it?"

"Yeah," I nodded and gulped at the same time.

"Okay let's get out before that big outside set gets here. Come on."

Mike stepped over the rail, pondered for just a moment, and jumped. In seconds he was paddling away, far from the jetty and those dangerous boulders.

Now it was my turn. It was too late to turn back so I carefully stepped over the rail and looked down at the ocean. It beckoned me as the ocean always beckons a surfer. A large swell was building about a hundred yards away. Should I wait? Mike was out in the lineup waving and yelling to hurry up. There was no time to think about it. I held my board up just as Mike had done and jumped. The water was cold but I was only under for a few seconds, jumping onto the surfboard as soon as possible, only to face a 10-foot swell not 20 yards away. After paddling over that swell another slightly bigger wall of water, towering at about 12 feet, followed right behind, maybe 10 seconds apart. But time was irrelevant at this point as I had been paddling frantically for about a minute now, and instead of moving away from the jetty I was being drawn closer to it with each new swell. I could hear Mike screaming from about 50 yards away but could not deal with the huge waves and strong currents.

Inevitably, it seemed I would be thrown against the rocks and crushed like a fly.

Now about 20 feet away from the jetty, with the weight of the situation becoming obvious and the very real possibility of not making it out alive, I came up with an idea; a strange one to be sure but the mere fact that my mind was still generating survival tactics at this point was encouraging.

I began paddling *towards* the jetty, thinking that if I could just get over to the rocks I could surely make my way back to the beach.

Getting to the rocks was no problem. Standing on them however would be slightly easier than running on ice in a pair of penny-loafers.

The feeling of being back on solid ground again, old terra firma, would be short-lived. Another large set was coming in and there was a real concern about being thrashed all over the rocks. Still there was hope.

'I can crawl under the jetty all the way to the beach,' was my thought. 'The water must be shallow in there. At least I won't drown.'

The situation was getting pretty REAL, and the choice between drowning and being thrown against the rocks had just been decided.

Once "inside" the jetty, this slightly crazy plan was looking like a success. The light could literally be seen at the end of the tunnel. Then a set came in. I could only watch in terror as the jetty became a rocky chamber filling up with water and heading toward me with the force of a hurricane. A vain attempt was made to outrun the wave, more out of panic and futility than for any other reason.

When the rushing water finally hit I sensed that this was it. I surely wouldn't survive this final onslaught.

First I was thrown down like a 155 lb. quarterback being slammed by Mean Joe Green of the Pittsburgh Steelers. Then the wave lifted me back up as the entire 'chamber' filled up with the sea's fury, carrying my helpless body about 20 feet and then once again depositing it on the slippery rocks.

Still alive and instinctively thinking of survival, I got up and, upon seeing the second wave of the set coming down my chamber of death, grabbed hold of one of the huge girders supporting the jetty with both arms, hanging on for dear life. Again the chamber filled with the powerful wave but this time the plan was working. Although submerged for what felt like forever, I was still clinging to that girder after the wave had past.

"Thank God!" I gasped. Then finally, at the top of tired lungs I yelled, "Help! Help! Somebody help!"

A few of the fishermen heard the calls.

"Hear that? Someone's yelling for help!"

"Yeah, but where is he?"

"Hey! There's a surfer under there!"

"HELP!!!"

"Don't worry man, we'll get you out of there!" a voice rang out from above like an answered prayer.

One of the fishermen was also a local surfer who thought the sea was too unforgiving that day to be paddling around on. He looked down through the steel storm grates strewn about two feet apart throughout the length of the jetty, and spotted my battered body clinging to a concrete girder waiting and praying for some kind of miracle.

The fisherman saw that I was standing two girders away from a steel ladder, one of two ladders leading from the deck of the jetty down into the inlet waters. He yelled from the storm grate directly above.

"Hey! There's a ladder over here! It's only two slabs away from you! Can you make it there?"

"Which way?" I asked, hanging on for dear life.

"Out to sea."

I surely didn't like the idea of moving into even deeper water but had to believe that this guy was going to get me out of this nightmare alive.

"I'll try!" was all I could say.

"Don't waste any time, bud. There's a set coming in about 30 seconds. I'll be waiting for you on the ladder!"

Hesitating for a couple of seconds, just enough to say one more short prayer, I let go of the girder that had kept me alive for the past few minutes and then made my way along the barnacle-covered boulders, finally stumbling into the next girder. Clinging to it just as I had the first one, I once again heard that ferocious sound of a big wave rushing through the first girders of the jetty about 20 yards away. This was getting old. Instead of waiting out another set clinging to the concrete structure for dear life, I made my move, let go and bailed off into the cold rushing water of the Sebastian Inlet.

About twenty feet away, standing on the ladder and dangling his t-shirt down over the water was the fisherman.

"Grab onto this!" he yelled. I grabbed hold of the t-shirt and both of us pulled until I was up the ladder and back on top of the jetty.

"Whew!" I said, and breathed a long sigh of relief. Had I not finally thought to call for help I would surely have been splattered all over the jetty rocks fifteen feet below where I now stood in awe, wondering how I was still alive and walking.

"Thanks a lot man," was the first thing I said to the young fisherman. We shook hands as he smiled and said to me, almost in disbelief,

"Man, I just saved your life!"

"You sure did. I'm sure glad you were here. Thanks again man, really."

"Anytime brother but you're crazy! What were you doing under there?"

"I guess I couldn't make it out into the lineup so I started swimming toward the jetty. Sounds kinda stupid I guess but I didn't know what else to do," I said, shrugging my shoulders.

Shivering, bloody, and in a state of shock, I could only think about getting home and dry, and had almost completely forgotten about Mike.

I limped down the jetty, passing the same fishermen that were standing there on my way out. They were all giving me strange looks and shaking their heads. One of them mumbled to another,

"Crazy surfers. Ain't they got no brains, Henry?"

"The ones that got brains don't come up here when it's like this, Frank."

As I got ever closer to the beach, one of them, perhaps Frank, asked me,

"Son, have you ever jumped off this pier before?"

"No sir."

"Well I don't mean to preach but there are some dangerous currents in this inlet, especially on a day like today. Those surfers out there know them like a swimming pool but you don't jump off THIS pier in these waves unless you know what you're doing! You're lucky to be alive, son!"

"Yes sir I am. I'm very lucky."

By the time I made it to the beach, Mike had gotten my board and was standing there waiting.

"You okay?" he asked. "I swam over and got your board before it could get smashed up. You're lucky, there isn't a scratch on it."

"Thanks Mike," I said, apathetically. My surfboard wasn't exactly top priority at that particular moment.

"You shouldn't have let go of your board. You should *never* let go of your board. Well, I'm going out to catch a few more. Are you coming?"

"Are you kidding?"

"Come on man, you'll get it right this time. Just jump right behind me instead of taking your own sweet time about it," Mike persisted.

"I don't think so. I'm taking off, man. See ya."

As I walked painfully back to the car I remember thinking about the future. I would live to see another day. At the dune line, before stepping down into the parking lot, I turned around to give the restless ocean one last look. It seemed so hard to believe that just 10 minutes earlier I had been fighting for my life under that jetty.

"Life is good," I thought. "Thank you, God."

A well known story in the Bible is the one in the New Testament where Jesus tells a few fishermen He will make them "fishers of men." Those who are unfamiliar with the way Jesus talks, thinks, and works in Scripture might have a difficult time figuring out what He meant by this, just as I did when first encountering the story in the Book of Matthew several years ago. Simply put, it means nothing more than the idea that if the fishermen would put down their nets and follow Him, He would teach them how to 'fish' other men (and women) out of a sea of darkness and lead them into the light of Christ.

When I first typed out this chapter long ago on a Brother typewriter, not too many years after my narrow escape from death at the Inlet, it was entitled simply "The Inlet." Stashed away for two decades in a large cardboard box, along with the nine other chapters of my very first manuscript **Hearts of Gold**, it kept that title for years. Eventually I succumbed to the technology of the 21st century, bought a computer, and transferred "The Inlet" into a digital file, where it safely remained for another few years. But when I decided to use the chapter in **A Spiritual Rebuild**, I re-read it and gave it one final edit before adding it to the rest of the planned manuscript. And I changed the name to "A Fisher of Men." The reason is because at first glance, this is the story of a young man who because of pride and foolishness gets caught in a situation that could easily have lead to serious injury or death. However, a second reading of the same chapter reveals a hidden meaning that can only be seen through the use of Scripture, specifically the New Testament verse pertaining to "fishers of men." It is, as Jesus was so fond of telling, a parable.

As Jesus might have explained it: The young man on the Sebastian Inlet jetty was out fishing in nasty weather (much like the fishermen in the Bible who were out in their boat when a storm came up) when out of the blue came a call for help. Jesus was telling him to put down his net, that there was a man who needed him more than the fisherman needed to fish. So the young man hurried over to the ladder on the jetty, took off his shirt and used it to literally "fish" the man in danger out of the ocean, and out of trouble. Whether that incident changed the fisherman's life that day or not, we will never know. He may have continued fishing for the rest of his life or he may have been inspired to become a firefighter or EMT, a nurse, doctor, or other lifesaver, maybe even a pastor. As I said, we will never know. But just as Jesus' disciples began changing lives, that fisherman surely changed mine, from death to life; from despair to sudden hope; and from unhappy to grateful for every minute. Did it turn me into an immediate Christ follower? Not immediately but time does not exist to God. Sure I stumbled and fell into the devious and cunning traps of Satan many many times since that incident at the Inlet forty years ago. But here I am today, a witness to the endless and wonderful amazing grace of God through faith in His beloved Son Jesus Christ. I am sure there are many past incidents in your life too, that if you re-examined them could be turned into parables that would be worthy of Jesus Himself telling them to His disciples.

5 FORSAKEN FOR BUT A MOMENT

There are times in life when it just doesn't seem like God is paying attention. We experience this almost daily on a global scale, but it happens to us on a personal basis as well. These are the times that put our faith to the test and separate the believers from the non-believers. And that's okay because it is important for us to know which category we belong in. God tests us on a daily basis, some days more so than others, because it is also important to Him which category we fall into. The Bible is rife with instances where God was seemingly nowhere to be found, to the point where the people would cry out in anguish waiting for a response. From Moses to Job to Jesus Himself, the most prolific leaders and characters in the Holy Bible at one time or another wondered if God had forsaken them. Not a single person has ever been spared His test of faith. So if you've taken a few too many hits on the chin lately, or sometimes feel defeated by life's constant battles, just know that you are never alone in that respect. For this is the human condition. As it is written in the Book of Isaiah (KJV):

"For a small moment have I forsaken thee; but with great mercies will I gather thee."

God has the power to forgive our sins and show us amazing grace through His only begotten Son Jesus Christ. This He does generously on a daily basis. But God also has the ultimate power to judge us and deliver His wrath and punishment liberally as He sees fit. This He can do through trials and tribulations on both an individual level and on larger populations, even on the global scale. But it doesn't mean God hates us just because we are punished. Just like a good father He takes us back under His wing and often, as in the Book of Isaiah, lavishes even more of His love and mercy upon us than ever before. Our God is an awesome God!

My life, like everyone else's, has had its fair share of trials and tribulations. There have been moments, days, weeks, months, even several years when I have sat contemplating on a boardwalk overlooking the Atlantic Ocean, one of the Creator's mighty bodies of water, looked out to sea, and wondered many things. Was there more to life than what I was experiencing? Was I being punished by God? Does God really speak to people and if so, why wasn't He speaking to me? I never questioned, at least since the age of about fifteen, the existence of God; I just didn't know how to get in touch with Him. By the age of 25 I had witnessed many of His miracles, yet at such a young age I never really appreciated everything He had done for me as an individual. Putting an end to the Viet Nam war should have been my first clue that God was looking out for all the guys in my neighborhood and in high school as well. That terrible war lasted from the early 1960's until 1973, one year before my older brother and his high school buddies would have been drafted into the military and shipped overseas to Southeast Asia. Several people I knew back then breathed a huge sigh of relief when the peace treaty was signed between the United States, South Viet Nam, the Viet Cong, and North Viet Nam. It was a senseless war that the United States had been stuck in for almost fifteen years. There was nothing romantic about it and by war's end most of the gung-ho patriotic attitude associated with Americans during wartime was non existent. The majority of Americans just wanted it to end. President Johnson admitted it on national television shortly before turning down the nomination for re-election in 1968. As a result, Richard Nixon won the election of '68 promising eventual peace and a long drawn out withdrawal of American soldiers from Southeast Asia. So when peace finally came, President Nixon was given almost full credit for his negotiating skills with the Chinese and their allies. Yet, as in the Old Testament of the Holy Bible, only God has the power to start and stop wars. So I believe the U.S. involvement in Southeast Asia in the 1960's was not in vain as many historians might have concluded. Rather, just as the U.S. has tried to keep peace in the Middle East and the rest of the world since the end of the Viet Nam war, the American military presence has always been portrayed as good vs. evil, with the good almost always prevailing. And I believe that as long as Americans choose the good side, we will always prevail in the end, because of God's desire to promote good over evil. In essence, I do believe that God is always in control, knows what is going on in this world at all times, and always has the power to destroy evil as He sees fit.

So I have seen miracles in my lifetime and I have also seen days when I wondered if God was punishing us, both individually and in groups. Natural disasters come to mind. Did He not tell Abraham in the Book of Genesis that He would not destroy a village as long as there were at least ten righteous people living there? Does that mean whenever a town is almost completely wiped off the map because of a hurricane, earthquake, volcano, etc. there were less than ten righteous people in that town? Perhaps no one prayed to God for the safety of the town prior to the disaster?

And then there were times when I wondered if I were being punished, simply because at the age of 26 life had not turned out quite the way I thought it was going to. Of course I had no clue how life was going to turn out because I never had a plan that included God until I reached middle age. As I had told my dad at a young age, my only plan at that time was to race motocross. When it became clear I wasn't going to earn a living at racing, there was no backup plan short of mowing grass for the rest of my days. With no backup plan and an instinctive attraction to members of the opposite sex yet still too shy to approach them, I was easy prey for any woman who fancied the thought of dating me. And that is exactly how I met my first wife. She thought I was 'cute', I found her attractive, she was five years older and BAM, a match made in heaven. Well it was for awhile until our relationship became more and more polarizing with each passing day. One day after work, with both of us sitting at the dinner table and our almost two-year-old daughter sitting in her high chair close by, my wife of two years told me that one of us had to leave. Well what was I supposed to say or do? I was 26 years old with about the same amount of wisdom as Wile E. Coyote chasing after the Road Runner on a Saturday morning cartoon in the 1960's. I couldn't just watch my wife and little girl walk out the door while I stayed in that empty house all alone.

We didn't own it anyway. So I offered to be the one to pack his bags, and moved back home with my dad, who had been living alone for almost ten years by that time. When I first told him about the situation over the phone, I thought he would practically disown me for leaving my wife and daughter, so I asked if I might stay with him for only a week until I could find somewhere else to stay. To my delight, he welcomed me back just like the *"man who had two sons"* in Jesus' parable about the prodigal son returning home in the Gospel of Luke Chapter 15:11-31 in the New Testament.

We got along pretty well. I was able to finish spreading my wings, and tried a few things that had been on my bucket list that may have never been possible had I not become single again. I missed my daughter terribly and second-guessed my decision to leave almost every waking moment of every single day. But whenever I tried to get back together with my ex, she always had a date lined up for the weekend so I knew she didn't want me anymore. Spiritually it was probably the saddest time in my life. The only thing that kept me going every day was the fact that I had to get up each morning and go to work to help support my daughter. As for myself, I didn't really want anything anymore. I tried a couple of times to get back into motocross racing but the drive just wasn't there. Of course there was still surfing, which was always a blessing. If I've said it once I'll say it again. There is nothing like surfing, especially soul surfing. A soul surfer is at peace with the world and one with the ocean, the waves, and in my case at least, God. He or she seeks nothing more while in the ocean than catching a nice wave and carving out a ride till it fades out or crashes on a sandbar or reef. It's the closest thing to a free ride I've ever found short of finding a nice hill on a bicycle and coasting all the way down, letting go of the handlebars for added effect. Whenever I wasn't mowing grass I was out in the water surfing. And there was a certain amount of unlimited freedom that I did enjoy while being a mower/surfer. At one point I decided to quit working at the golf course altogether and simply mow grass and surf. Bought a 1967 Dodge window van and decided to give old Dad a break by practically living and working out of that old van. It was pretty fun, I won't lie; mowing grass every day until the sun went down; or if I'd heard or thought the surf might be up I'd mow until there were only a couple hours daylight left, and then park the van in a secret spot in the palmettos by the beach and go surfing until the sun went down. Then I'd throw the board in the back of the van with the mower, weedeater, and blower, go grab something to eat or, depending upon how late it was, just light up the mosquito repellant, climb onto the mattress behind the driver's seat, and fall asleep listening to the gentle lapping of the ocean's waves on the shore about thirty yards away. It wasn't a bad life, until the van broke down one day. She just quit; needed some serious work so I sold it to a buddy who thought he could fix it and I never saw it again. Since I was still living at home, Dad gave me his old AMC Hornet to use and then later just said it was mine. I still couldn't believe he was proud of me after all I had been through and the way I was disrupting his life. He never came right out and said he was proud but his family was not the kind of people who told you what they thought. He came from a farming family in Manitou, Manitoba, Canada. They worked hard for every penny they ever had, and I guess he could see that I was turning into that kind of a person myself. If there ever was any doubt in his mind before, he could tell by then that I was truly his son. And that made us both feel proud.

After two full years of living back home with Dad I was ready to start out on my own again and get back on my feet as they say. Dad was actually sad that I was leaving, and I didn't really want to leave but I knew I had to. A man can never grow up if he never leaves home. And while leaving home for the second time opened up a whole new set of problems, I know it was God's will, His way of eventually leading me back to Him. Yes God has been with me all the way, throughout my life, even when I had no idea that He was watching. Yet as the chapter title suggests, there was one time when I thought, if only for a moment, that He had either given up on me or I had slipped off his radar. It was a moment I will never forget. I could have awakened from it to find myself in the midst of Hell because my life at that time had no firm roots in Jesus Christ. Instead when I awoke I began to shun everything that was evil and bad. It was the turning point that would eventually lead me to having the desire to give my life to Christ. It didn't happen overnight; I admit to still being a 'baby Christian.' But I am growing more in Christ with each passing day, and I believe the big change happened at this turning point, which I will do my best to describe as much as I can recollect.

It was during the Christmas season of 1986. I had met a girl about 23 years old at a bar in my hometown. We started dating and everything was going pretty well for a few weeks. Then I began to notice a change in her. We both drank a little too much whenever we went out and she began to turn mean, I guess you could say bipolar, whenever she had too much to drink. Not having any background in psychology back then I didn't know anything about bipolar people. It just seemed strange that a person could be so lovey-dovey one minute and then turn on me like a mad dog the next. One evening after a nice dinner at a restaurant in my hometown, we were both pretty wobbly as we walked through the parking lot toward my old van. As we got closer to it she started getting mean, just as she had on a couple of previous occasions. I can't even remember the dialogue as it was crazy anyway. All I know is she lied down on the pavement, just as she had done once before, and demanded that I pick her back up. And just as I had done the first time, I reached down and tried to pick her up off the ground. Well the first time it happened a few weeks before, I had convinced her that she was drunk and that I needed to pick her up and take her home. And it worked. But this time when I reached down to pull her up she grabbed hold of my arms and yanked me down, and I fell face first, the corner of my left eye slamming against a concrete parking curb. As I lay down on the asphalt beside her, moaning and lamenting that I didn't want to live anymore, I guess she snapped out of it because she got up, looked down at me and thought I was dying. And then I heard her say,

"Oh no, what am I going to tell my parents? They're going to kill me! I know, I'll tell them he got hit by a golf ball on the golf course. Yeah! That's what I'll tell them."

It was at that moment I finally realized she didn't give a crap about me. Her only concern was hoping her parents would never find out the truth. With blood leaking out of a deep wound on the corner of my eye, I suddenly sobered up, and I swear that is when the Holy Spirit must have entered my body to lead me out of that whole mess. I quickly got up, walked over to my old van and hopped in behind the wheel. She followed behind me and opened the passenger side door and, reverting back to her alter ego, said she wasn't coming with me.

"Fine," I said. "Then get out."

She looked surprised that I wasn't begging her to stay in the van so I could take her home. But I was serious so she climbed up into the passenger seat and I drove her home. I never dated her again. Life is too short to get involved with people who only pretend to care about you.

As for me, my eye took awhile to heal. My boss at the golf course was compassionate to the point of being amazing. The company let me work in the paint shop for a couple months, painting mowers and tractors and doing odd jobs so that my wound could stay somewhat clean. I think they were kind of surprised that a guy would even come to work with a big bandage on his head by his eye every day. But my work was my life. It kept me focused and kept me from thinking about my daughter, whose mother had moved her up to Tennessee to live with the guy whom she eventually married and bore another child with.

I didn't stop messing up. I still needed to curb my drinking habits. That would happen a few months later when I got pulled over and charged with a DUI; another lesson learned. Thanks be to God that no one has died and I have been the only one injured by the lack of good judgment in the past. I was about to turn 30 in a couple months and felt as though I was finally gaining some much needed wisdom. Sure, it was only the tip of a large iceberg, but I would enter my third decade with more knowledge of life, work, and women, three subjects that I had always tried to learn more about. I was not yet familiar with God, Jesus, or the Holy Spirit, but I knew deep down inside that He had a purpose for me. There was no way He would have brought me through so many pitfalls if He didn't have a better plan for me someday. And that gave me hope for the future.

I continued to hope and pray each day that I would get to see my daughter again somehow. It had been about a year since she and her mom left for Tennessee, and I had no clue as to whether or not they would ever move back down to Florida. It was a sad situation I had gotten myself into and now that they were in another state I realized how powerless I was concerning the fate of my only child. I decided to give her up to God, and prayed that He would watch over her since I had lost contact with her. My prayer was answered in such a way that brought the joy back into my heart like nothing else could have. I got a call one day from my brother asking me to come over to his house, there was someone there who wanted to see me. I swear I had no clue who it might be. After all, friends and relatives had come down in the past to visit and I thought it might be someone from my distant past. Well it was someone from my past alright. My ex had brought my daughter to my brother's house to surprise me because she didn't know where I was living at the time. What a surprise! Words cannot even begin to describe how happy I was to see that little girl again. I vowed right then and there I would do everything I could to keep her from moving away again, no matter how hard I had to work. There was still no way of getting back together with my ex as she had just had another baby, a little boy, and there was no way the boy's daddy was going to give him or my ex up just to make me happy. Things were still far from perfect but my daughter's return to Florida was not only a huge blessing but also an answered prayer. Giving my daughter up to God was the best thing I ever did for both of us. In Scripture, Matthew 7:7 (NIV) says it best:

"Ask and it will be given to you; seek and you will find; knock and the door will be opened to you."

6 THE FIRST REBUILD

When the year 1988 began I was in the last few months of my twenties. If you've been there before or are very close to that self-imposed milestone, it *feels* like old age is waiting just around the bend. Funny, we couldn't wait to turn 21 but turning 30 felt like we were losing everything we had cherished about our youth; as if all the good times, the innocence, the best things in life would be nothing but memories to share with our childhood friends when we got together again. In reality turning 30 means only what one allows it or wants it to mean. The only population or group that may actually be affected by turning 30 are professional athletes. Studies have shown that humans on average begin to slow down once they reach 30 or shortly thereafter. But it is largely a slow and gradual process like life itself. To the rest of us, 30 remains just one year older than 29. But don't try telling that to a 29 year-old-going-on 30.

At 29 I was divorced, single, and trying to live on my own while helping to support my 4 year-old daughter. Still working on the same golf course since the age of 19, it felt like I had the spirit of an old man. The men on the crew came and went over the years; I would guess the average length of employment was probably around three or four years. After seven years or so you start feeling like you are one of the old men of the golf course, almost a part of the scenery. Seasons come and seasons go. Every year around spring time there is a sense of renewal. The winter rye grass dies off and with the April showers comes the lush green growth of summertime. And with each summer comes the reality that the heat will be here for another six months because that's how it is in Florida: six months of almost unbearable heat followed by six months of really nice weather, including some nearly perfect days and nights. Wintertime in Florida is the best time to do *everything*. If I had a dime for every time I have ever said or heard the phrase *"I could stand it if the weather was like this year 'round"*, I could probably retire tomorrow and do nothing but write books and go hiking and mountain biking in the Georgia hills. But then there are the summers. I haven't traveled much in my lifetime but if there are hotter places on Earth than Florida in mid-September I don't care to go there and I sure wouldn't want to work there, outdoors anyway. But golf course work was not bad, in fact I kind of enjoyed it. I mean, how else could I have stayed in the same job for ten years, right? There is something to be said for working in the great outdoors no matter the weather or how cliché it sounds. Riding out onto the course every morning as the sun rises over the trees; being the first one to walk on the dew-covered Bermuda grass, leaving fresh footprints behind like walking in the snow; the solitude of man and machine helping to re-create a beautiful landscape out of just sand and grass; there is no question about the spiritual aspect of golf course maintenance. It never really gets old unless one works on the same course for several years. Then, like every other job it becomes too routine, and one longs for some type, *any type* of change. So it was for me after ten years of mowing greens, tees, fairways, and roughs on the same golf course for ten years. In the spring of '88 change was in the air. I could feel it in my bones. Something was going to happen to break up the routine. However, there is a caveat in asking for change, and it is this: Be careful what you ask for because you might get it. Ever heard the old saying, "Out of the frying pan and into the fire"? It literally means that if you are not going to change things for the better, you'd be better off leaving well enough alone.

Case in point: Change did come that spring, in the form of a fellow high school alumnus looking for someone to replace his long-time dependable lawn maintenance worker who had just quit with only a couple days' notice. As I was driving down a fairway one day on the tee mower, he came dashing out of the rough from a client's backyard, waving his arms to grab my attention. Thinking he might be in some kind of trouble I headed over to him and shut the engine down. I recognized him instantly as one of the standout players on our high school football team at my alma mater. He wore an old straw hat, a brown tee-shirt, and brown hospital scrub pants. *"Well that's different"* I thought. I could tell he was really busy by his demeanor and the way he spoke without much pause.

"Hey, would you be interested in working for me? My main guy just quit and it's just me and my dad. I offer two weeks of vacation with pay, paid holidays, insurance, and I pay overtime on Saturdays. If you're interested here's my number. Think about it and give me a call. Well, I've gotta get back to work. Give me a call if you're interested."

And he walked off through the rough and back into the yard where he had come from. So I cranked up the tee mower and headed back down the fairway to the next set of tees. Hmmmm. Something to think about.

It didn't take long to make a decision. Upon calling up my brother after work that day (not everyone had cell phones back then) and getting his opinion on the opportunity, I then called my prospective boss and told him I would accept his job offer. He was delighted. I had a week to say goodbye to my old friends and co-workers at the golf course prior to working on my first full-time lawn maintenance crew. Until then lawn maintenance had been a part-time venture for me, a way to make extra money, which was very scarce at the time. Except for the year I set out on my own with a Snapper® self-propelled 26-inch mower, a weedeater, blower, and an old '67 Dodge window van, I had been mowing only a couple yards each day following 8 hours of golf course maintenance work. Being driven by a former high school football defensive tackle and West Point Academy graduate to mow 60 yards per week with his dad turned out to be my first spiritual rebuild. We mowed every week (let's see if I can get this right) twenty yards every Monday, sixteen on Tuesday, twelve on Wednesday, Eight bigger ones on Thursday and four humongous yards every Friday. At first I thought with that many yards I would be hard-pressed to continue mowing the half-dozen or so yards that remained in my part-time portfolio. Was I ever wrong! My new boss was even busier than I was in his 'spare time', as he was also an assistant football coach for a local high school. Talk about ambitious! Turns out he had aspirations of coaching college football one day, when he could afford to retire from the lawn business. By the way, that dream did eventually come true.

The first summer of my 'new life' was 'a real bear' as my boss would often say. The contrast between lawn maintenance and golf course maintenance was even more than I had anticipated, especially the mowing part. Mowing grass on the golf course was probably one of the most enjoyable jobs one could do outdoors, since it almost always consisted of utilizing the latest in golf course industry technology, which in the 1980's meant riding mowers with hydraulic drive motors and comfortable seats. We were one of the few courses that still used walk-behind mowers for the greens, but most of us found that to be quite an enjoyable job as well. Mowing grass during the summer in the lawn maintenance business using mowers with anything but hydraulic drive was extremely hard work. Reason being that during the summer months in Florida the dew is really heavy in the mornings and it used to saturate the belts on the 36-inch belt-driven mowers we were using, to the point that they could no longer be considered self-propelled. If you've never had the experience of trying to push a 36-inch 16hp 450lb lawn mower around a yard filled with 6-inch high, thick dark green St. Augustine freshly fertilized grass, stopping every 30 feet or so to dump the full grass catcher, well then you haven't missed anything that you will regret later. All of that in the sweltering 95-100 degree heat and 101% humidity and with the Florida sun beating down so hot you could see it radiating off both the grass and the pavement in the distance. Let's just put it this way: At the age of 62, with my lung capacity, physical strength, older joints, and willpower roughly two-thirds at best of what it was 32 years ago, half my life, I still might consider, if I had to, working on a golf course; especially if the scenery were totally awesome, as it is in the hills of Georgia and North Carolina. As for going back to working on a lawn maintenance crew, I doubt I could ever do it full-time anymore; maybe part-time or at my own pace but not in the bust-ass world of a real lawn maintenance crew. Even in the winters it's tough. The weather is just about perfect for the most part but you're not really getting to enjoy it. Spreading mulch, digging out split-leaf philodendrons, cutting back bougainvillea bushes, and other tasks that are always left to the 'gardeners' ensure that even the winter months can be less than tolerable to someone who is used to overseeding golf course greens, tees, and fairways and driving around on a tractor vacuuming up leaves all winter.

The second season working for my boss/coach was thankfully not as tough as the first one, or perhaps I had become tougher. I like the way the King James Version of the Bible states it in Proverbs 27:17.

Iron sharpeneth iron; so a man sharpeneth the countenance of his friend.

And indeed the football coach/West Point grad was 'sharpening' me the best way he knew how, by making me tougher. I was thirty years old but much tougher and stronger than I had ever been, including the year I raced the Florida AMA summer series at the age of 21. My only regret is that I did not know Jesus yet. If I would have known him back then there is no telling what I might have done with my life. As it was, with my new and first spiritual rebuild, I was able to work more efficiently and have more confidence in everything I did. My boss taught me to persevere in all my endeavors, both on the job and off. I bought a used dirt bike, an '85 Honda CR250 Elsinore, and rode the wheels off it whenever my old buddy John and I would go riding, with more strength, more spirit and enthusiasm, and more courage than I had in 1980 during the AMA series. Of course it had a lot to do with the bike too. The '85 Elsinore 250 was the best handling bike I had ever owned. Compared to my '79 it was a dream machine that I likely never would have bought if not for my spiritual rebuild. Even the mower wasn't as hard to push during that second season. In order to combat fatigue from fighting with it every day, I had started a training regimen that must have even made my boss wonder how I was getting so much stronger in such little time. It began in the spring of that year, the best time to start any new project. I would get up every morning during the week at 4:30 and have a little breakfast; by 5:00 I was ready for my daily workout: barbell presses, bench presses, situps, curls, power cleans, and some chest pulls with a chest expander device. By mid-summer I reached the pinnacle of strength for my whole life. Even I couldn't believe I was so strong. My boss was proud of me and I was proud of myself. And yet, just as Scripture says, pride usually precedes a downfall.

Pride goes before destruction,

a haughty spirit before a fall.

Better to be lowly in spirit along with the oppressed

than to share plunder with the proud.

Proverbs 16: 18-19

With newfound strength and the body to go with it I was strutting around all summer with no shirt. And since I never wore sunscreen except on my face, even when I'd go surfing, it was only a matter of time before the sun's dangerous rays turned my freckled outer covering into a breeding ground for skin cancer. It started as a hyper-sensitive painful growth in the middle of my back and ended with the surgical removal of squamous-cell carcinoma the size of a quarter about an inch deep into my back. And what really stung was when the dermatologist recommended I never go outside again without a long sleeve shirt, long pants, and a wide-brimmed hat, or the equivalent coverage of sun block, 50+ SPF. For someone who hated to smear any kind of healing oils on his skin, that wasn't even an option I had ever considered. In effect, my life had been drastically altered once again. I began to consider what types of indoor jobs I might be able to do besides working in a kitchen. I hadn't even thought of praying about it, as I didn't pray that much in those days until one night.....

It was at the end of another long day. Having been up since 4:30am doing exercises followed by eight hours of work in my boss's yards and then a couple of my own customers', I was exhausted. And I had a headache that wouldn't go away. My dad had given me a bottle of 222 pills from his medicine cabinet. Don't know how he got them or when, as they were supposedly a Canadian pill with codeine, which was not available over the counter in the U.S. But Dad said they worked great for taking away pain, especially headaches, and he should've known, as he often suffered from debilitating migraines. So that night I took a couple right before hitting the sack. I don't think I have described my little apartment on the beach yet so I will do so now; it won't take long. It was a one room efficiency with a bathroom, shower, and small kitchenette. When you walked in the door you pretty much saw everything I had to my name that wasn't in the closet. And about the only thing I kept in the closet besides clothes was my surfboard.

I guess it was around about midnight. My headache seemed to be going away and I was about to fall into a sound sleep when out of the blue I felt a sharp pain in my abdominal area. It became so severe I thought I was having a heart attack and began praying to God, asking Him to either take this terrible pain away or to take me. Since I wasn't familiar with Scripture back then I didn't even think to pray for forgiveness of my sins, which is what I should have done if I wanted any chance of entering the gates of Heaven. It was Jesus who taught his disciples how to pray using the Lord's Prayer as a guideline, and then followed up with this:

"For if you forgive other people when they sin against you, your heavenly father will also forgive you. But if you do not forgive others their sins, your Father will not forgive your sins." -

Matthew 6:14-15 (NIV)

To my amazement, after what felt like about an hour of writhing in pain, twisting and turning in bed, feeling like someone was jabbing a knife into my stomach and cutting it up, the pain subsided just as quickly as it had come about. A great feeling of relief came over me, much like a pregnant woman must feel when her newborn's feet finally exit the birth canal. I sat up in my bed and thanked the Lord. Usually when I thanked the Lord it had always been a 'Thank you God' moment and that was it. But this time was different. It may sound trite but I felt the Lord's presence; I mean I *knew* the Lord, the Holy Spirit, or an angel was standing in front of me not ten feet away. It couldn't have been any further than that because my bed was only about ten feet opposite the closet across the room. I *knew* He was there; so much so that after about five minutes of sitting in His presence I asked out loud,

"Lord, are you there?"

To my recollection the Spirit remained in my room for about ten minutes. For those ten minutes I felt such a peace within my soul that I was wondering if He was going to take me at that time or even if I had already died from a heart attack and my soul was waiting for Jesus to take me up to Heaven. But the blissful feeling of an overwhelming peace went away, as did the presence of the Holy Spirit, and I was left sitting on the edge of the bed wondering what had just happened. The next morning I got up and went to work as usual but there was no doubt I had been changed once again as God continued to put me through the necessary 'adjustments' to prepare me for the rest of my life and eternity as well. I had learned two things from the experience: First, I was indeed mortal and old enough to start being more concerned about my health. Even with all the physical activity I endured every single day, I was still prone to heart attacks and every other malady that human beings get concerned about once they reach their thirties. Secondly, there was now no doubt in my mind that God could send His Holy Spirit down to help us whenever we call on Him or whenever He knows we really need Him. And the Holy Spirit is **real**.

If you've never felt the presence of God, Jesus, or the Holy Spirit, pray that He visits you sometime. And don't wait until you think it might be your last few moments on the planet. For it is written:

Those who live according to the flesh have their minds set on what the flesh desires; but those who live in accordance with the Spirit have their minds set on what the Spirit desires. The mind governed by the flesh is death, but the mind governed by the Spirit is life and peace. - Romans 8:5-6 (NIV)

7 SECOND REBUILD – THE PLAN

As the old saying goes, "This too shall pass," and after my second full year of working for the West Point grad he announced that he would be selling the lawn business and moving on to bigger and better things. He had had enough of those sweltering summer days when one's t-shirt would be soaking wet by around 9:00 in the morning and stay that way until quitting time each day. He had at first assumed that I would be staying on with the new owner, until I assured him that I had no interest in giving it my all every day if he wasn't going to be there too. After all, he had never missed a day of work since I started that job. I didn't even know what it would be like to take care of all those yards without his unrelenting motivation. No, I had decided from the first moment I heard about my boss selling the business that I would have to find a new line of work.

About a week after my boss found out that I wouldn't be staying on, we were sitting on a client's front lawn to eat our lunches, just as we did every day around 11:30. Sitting cross-legged across from each other on the freshly-mowed green grass, he asked me what I would be doing for work after the business sold. It was reminiscent of the way my dad used to sit me down in the Florida Room of our old home and ask what I was going to be when I grew up; only this time I had been giving it some thought, and it wasn't some kid's dream of racing motocross for a living.

"I've been doing some research, and I think I'll go back to school and learn how to shoot X-rays," I said. "I've always thought that would be pretty cool."

"Hmm," said my boss. "X-ray school, huh? Sounds like you've got it all figured out Rickster. Don't you need to get some kind of school loan for that?"

"Well, I figure if I can get a job at the hospital doing something, you know, get my foot in the door, maybe they will pay for X-ray school."

My boss then reached over to where his straw hat lay on the grass by his feet, grabbed it and plopped it on top of his head. Lunchtime was over, time to get back to work. As we both stood up he nodded and said,

"X-rays, huh? Sounds good Rick."

And we cranked up our machines and got back to work.

And that was the plan. Everything fell into place at first. I got my foot in the door at our local hospital as a "sterile prep tech" which, like virtually everyone else, I had never even heard of before. The great news was my hunch was correct; the hospital would pay for all schooling. All I would have to do after passing all the prerequisite courses was to get accepted into X-ray school or as it was called, the radiography program.

Now you might be wondering how in the world the idea of shooting x-rays would enter into the mind of someone who had been mowing grass and maintaining golf courses for the well-to-do during the previous twelve years since graduating from high school. Though it may seem a bit strange and completely by chance, there was a certain amount of logic involved. You see, as I grew older and repeatedly witnessed the miracles of God's saving grace as He helped me stumble through life's challenges and pitfalls, I inevitably became wiser, though much slower than I might have hoped for. And with wisdom came the desire to actually try to please God, a notion that was quite novel to me at the time. Remember I was not raised a devout Christian although my parents definitely had good solid values. With very little knowledge of Scripture or the grace of God, I thought it possible to somehow *repay* God for everything I had done wrong thus far in life. One thing I knew for certain was that God does not want us to covet anything, worship false idols, or love money. You know we had no internet back then, but I had read that in the Bible somewhere. I figured that up to that point most of my life's work had been helping to beautify golf courses for the benefit of people who coveted money. And I was pretty sure that God would not want me to devote my whole life to that end. That was when I decided to find a career that He might be pleased with. I had been a hospital patient and gone to the emergency room for x-rays quite a few times by then and had always found it interesting, kind of like photography with a medical twist. How hard could it be?

Do yourself a favor and never ask that question because you will find out sooner or later how hard it can actually be. First of all, I don't want to say anything to discourage *anyone* from going back to school at *any time* during your life. Attending college and earning my two degrees have been some of the best years of my life, and I am so glad that I made the decision to return even later at the age of 45 to complete a Bachelor's in Psychology. Even though I never made a career out of psychology, the studying, discipline, critical thinking and *writing* involved in achieving any Bachelor's degree is enough to expand one's scholastic skills and instill confidence in one's ability to succeed at any task at hand. Yet I don't want to jump out too far ahead here and "put the carriage before the horse," as my dad used to say. The Bachelor's degree would not come until 2007, fifteen years after my first class in what we used to call *community college.* All around the state of Florida, they are now called state colleges, a great way to complete the first two years of a Bachelor's degree. Smaller classrooms and less expensive tuition make for a more student-friendly environment for college freshmen and sophomores. But state colleges also serve another purpose as they often double as two-year technical schools for applied science degree-seeking students and others who wish to transfer directly from one or two years of schooling into the trade of their choice. My choice was the two-year Radiography program, set up to be completed in a two-year time span for full-time students. As a full-time sterile prep tech at our hospital, I elected to complete what was (and probably still is) known as the *prerequisite* classes prior to applying for acceptance into the program.

So after my hard-working lawn maintenance boss and I said our goodbyes and put in one last week of our 60 homes/week responsibility to the wealthy people living on the intracoastal waterway, I went home to a small apartment by the beach and awaited the call that would hopefully soon come from the human resources department at the hospital. It turned out to be another crossroads in my life where God intervened but, since I wasn't a praying man yet, I had no idea whatsoever which direction He wanted me to go. You see, when my family found out that I was leaving the lawn business for greener pastures, they planted the idea in my head that I might consider becoming a firefighter like my older brother. And it got me thinking. And I thought, you know, that might be a viable choice, a great idea even. So I told my brother I was interested. Not only was he excited but the whole family was so happy at the prospect of my brother and I working together in the fire department. But they put me on hold for three whole months while I was out of work with little money in reserve. And the idea that was planted in my head three months earlier had to be put aside for the almost sure thing at the hospital. As Jesus said in the parable of the farmer sowing seed in the book of Luke:

"Some fell on rocky ground, and when it came up, the plants withered because they had no moisture."
Luke - 8:6
"Those on the rocky ground are the ones who receive the word with joy when they hear it, but they have no

root. They believe for awhile, but in the time of testing they fall away." Luke - 8:13

Having no knowledge of scripture at that time, I had no idea I was being tested by God to see how deep my desire was to be a firefighter. Unlike my brother, who lived and breathed the firefighting life, the dream of fighting fires had no real roots in my heart and soul. I had simply thought it would be great to work with my brother in a career that *he* loved. God doesn't want us to choose our lives or careers in accordance with what others might choose for us or themselves. It is His desire that we each find our own pathway that makes us happy, fulfills our role in this life and leads us back to Him.

"For I know the plans I have for you," declares the Lord, "plans to prosper you and not to harm you, plans to give you hope and a future."

Jeremiah 29:11

When the hospital finally called I was ecstatic, so excited to be starting out in a brand new career, a career with a future that did not include mowing grass or working outdoors in the sweltering heat of the Florida summers. The plan was to secure an entry level position that would enable me to work full-time while going to college to complete a two-year degree in radiography, or x-ray technology. The department I would work in while completing that degree was called (at that time) sterile prep. It is now known around the state of Florida as sterile processing. It was and still is a department that exists in virtually every hospital that performs surgery with reusable sterile instruments. The sterile processing technician position has many different job descriptions throughout the country, but a tech's main job has always been to provide sterile instruments to the operating room for surgery each day. It's not an easy task, nor is it the most enjoyable job I've ever had to do, but it got my foot in the door for a potential future in the medical field. I could go a lot deeper into the subject of sterile processing but one of the reasons this book is entitled **Volume III** instead of **Volume II** is because I have already written a book about sterile processing that covers my career in the field from 1990 through the present day. Thus, having already covered the details of what I was doing in the hospital while taking prerequisite courses in college for the x-ray program, I can just cut to the chase and begin with my acceptance into the program.

As I had said to my old boss in the lawn business, I found radiology to be a fascinating subject. The science of *shooting* a beam through a patient's body and producing a picture, or radiographic image, was definitely something I was looking forward to learning. I counted getting accepted into the radiography program as one of the highlights of my life and the first one that actually could have given me a great future. There were so many facets and possibilities in the career. And it continues to develop even today with more advanced equipment and technology. The biggest question would be: Could I adapt to a world where I would be a caregiver responsible for sick patients, sometimes very sick; or was I even cut out for that sort of thing? Only time would tell.

There were a couple of preliminary courses to get through before our class of twelve students would get the opportunity to do clinical rotations in the hospital. We learned all about x-rays, from physics to their history.

There was a course on medical terminology that taught all the vocabulary, or medical jargon, used in the field. There was a mock x-ray examining table in the classroom complete with an authentic radiographic arm, and a chest x-ray backboard on the wall as well. By the time they cut us loose in the hospitals in groups of four, we more or less knew what to expect or at least we thought we did. It was funny how much one could change in a matter of weeks just by a change of focus. Two months into clinicals and we all looked the part of medical professionals with our white lab coats, neat haircuts, and carrying our pocket-size notebooks around wherever we went. One of our professors informed us that a true x-ray technologist has "x-ray vision", meaning that he or she could look at a person and judge the size of his or her lungs and where they were situated in relation to their ribs; how big a patient's bones are so the technologist could tell how much force to use with the x-ray machine; and various other signs that were useful when setting up for radiographic exams. It gave us something to shoot for as well as another way to tell how quickly we were improving our skills. Of course other people we came in contact with may have thought we were looking at them a little strange or staring a bit too long, but that was in the mid-1990's and people weren't quite as suspicious of other folks back then as they are in the 2020's. Three months into the program I realized that my second spiritual rebuild was going to be more than just a tweak, as the first one had been. Changing from a golf course maintenance worker into a lawn maintenance worker had been a big change, but mostly because the job was a lot tougher physically. As I illustrated, pretty well I thought, in the book **Mowing at the Master's Level** (2018), once you've learned the basics about mowing grass, with a little practice you could probably mow any kind of grass anywhere on the planet. On the other hand, morphing into a radiographer from a golf course/lawn maintenance worker was more than just a spiritual rebuild, it was more like an overhaul. Luckily by that time I had already been working in the hospital for 4 years as a sterile prep tech. That definitely worked in my favor, at least at first, as most of the other students in my class had never even worked in the medical field before, so a hospital setting was totally new to them. One of my student cohorts had been my lab partner in anatomy/physiology class so we naturally became pretty good buds during the program. We'd go to parties together, study together, go to the college gym together, and generally just try to help each other get through the x-ray program. But it was still a tough program and he had to drop out after the first semester of clinicals as his grades hadn't been up to our professor's high standards. So the second semester would be all business, not nearly as fun as the first one had been with my buddy in the program. And of course it was more difficult. With each successive semester we learned more complex positions and more patient-intensive procedures as well. During the first semester our biggest hurdle as a group was that we each had to comp on a barium enema study. Of course none of us looked forward to that. Not many hospitals even use that procedure anymore since the widespread use of flexible endoscopes. But it was the mid-1990's and flexible scopes were not used in all hospitals so we had to know how to perform a barium enema. I should still be able to recite the steps in the exam since I used it as my mid-term assignment, which was to choose a radiographic procedure and present it to the class, using notes and actual radiographs from an exam. My presentation went really well; the class was pretty impressed that someone would actually use a barium enema for his or her mid-term assignment. The professor liked it too, and called me 'Professor Hughes' when I was finished with the presentation. That I will never forget. It sounded good and went well with the long white lab coat I chose to wear for clinicals. Yet the exam itself did not go quite as smoothly as the final presentation might have indicated. The second semester brought more challenges, just as it should have. But by then I was really questioning whether or not radiography was going to be my chosen career. Had I prayed on it and asked for God's guidance, I might have known for sure what to do. But praying had not been part of my daily practice back then so everything I did was just hit or miss. Scripture says that a man may choose his path but the Lord guides his steps. Without even knowing Scripture, I was unwittingly letting the Lord guide my steps. He was already slowly steering me away from the radiography program; it wasn't my destiny. I think the icing on the cake was when one of my co-workers in sterile prep told me one day that I might be seeing her dad the next day in the x-ray department as he was to undergo several tests to rule out clogged arteries or veins or something similar. The procedure included filling certain blood vessels with radiographic dye prior to viewing them on a monitor while the radiologist recorded the results. True to my co-worker's prediction I was told by my clinical instructor that there was an elderly gentleman on a gurney in the hallway next to the examining room who was waiting to be transferred into the room for his exam. He was already hooked up to IV's on a pole at the head of the gurney, via approximately 4 to 6 lines leading to several IV pumps. I asked the patient his name per protocol to see if the name on his wristband matched. I noticed he was in his eighties and it hit me that this was probably my co-worker's beloved dad. I asked him how he was feeling and he sounded kind of grumpy. Then I told him I was going to wheel him into the exam room so that his doctor could give him an exam. He said okay so I began pushing the gurney. When I did, the patient gave out a loud yell like I was hurting him. I had forgotten to move the IV pole with the gurney, and all the needles taped to his arms almost got yanked out of their veins. Needless to say I felt terrible. I told my clinical instructor what had just happened so that someone could check to see if any of the needles got ripped out of the patient's arm. He told me not to worry about it and that it happens a lot with students, but I still felt horrible.

After that incident I really wasn't sure if I still wanted to be a radiographer and I lost my focus. Luckily the semester was almost over and I once again passed clinicals with flying colors; but the writing was on the wall. The following semester would focus on radiography of the skull; extremely complex, requiring 100% focus on both the books and clinicals; not to mention I was still working full-time on the evening shift (3-11) at the same hospital where I would be doing clinicals during the next semester. That turned out to be the straw that broke the camel's back. I just could not handle spending 8 hours in clinicals each day and going to work each night until 11:00. I was going stir crazy in that place, on top of everything else. One of the techs had a party at his house on a Saturday night and invited the students so I went, thinking it might be a great way to let off some steam with everyone else. Well I ended up drinking too much and made a jerk out of myself instead. When one of my professors heard about it he called me into his office and told me I was now walking a thin line and he could kick me out of the program anytime he felt like it. Well that did it; pushed me over the limit. I walked out of his office, told myself I would never step foot in a radiology department or classroom again, and never looked back. It was over.

8 DISAPPOINTMENT

I remember driving to the Sebastian Inlet, one of my favorite spots on the planet back then, walking down the long boardwalk and just sitting on the wooden railing for about an hour watching the waves roll in. It wasn't so unusual for me to meditate at the beach in those days; on the contrary I loved gathering my thoughts by the ocean. But that day was different. I was supposed to be at the hospital doing clinicals in the radiography program, as I had been doing for about a year without missing a single class. My future had been all mapped out for me by the college, the hospital, and myself; that is until the instructor gave me an ultimatum, which finally drove me over the edge, and now I just didn't care anymore. That was on Friday. And there I sat on Saturday, the next day, on the boardwalk at the Inlet not knowing what to do now that my whole future had just vanished before my very eyes. Five years of working, studying, planning, and dreaming of graduating college with a degree in radiography; down the tubes, as we used to say. And I didn't have a clue what to do next. So I just did what came naturally to me in a situation like that: sat there staring at the waves. Maybe one of them would have the answer I was looking for.

And yet it was all so confusing, the way everything was going along so smoothly throughout the prerequisite classes, getting A's and B's in science classes when I hated science back in high school; acing college algebra exams like I was some kind of math wiz; and then being accepted into the radiography program with such high hopes. It seemed obvious that God had been leading me the whole way up to that point. But why did He not lead me *through it*? There were so many questions. As I look back on the whole situation 25 years later as a more mature Christian, some of the answers are turning up in Scripture as I learn more about God and Jesus Christ. As you read in the last chapter, "Second Rebuild - The Plan", the greatest disservice I did to myself in terms of completing x-ray school and becoming a full-fledged radiography tech was that I had lost faith. Things weren't going as smoothly as I would have liked and so I lost the faith and confidence that had gotten me that far in the first place. And what does the Bible say about faith?

The apostle Paul wrote:

But he (The Lord) said to me, "My grace is sufficient for you, for my power is made perfect in weakness."

- 2 Corinthians 12:9

Proverbs 3:5-6 tells us to:

Trust in the Lord with all your heart and lean not on your own understanding; in all your ways submit to Him and He will make your paths straight.

Had I known how to pray my way through trouble and indecision back then, the results might have been considerably different. Yet even though I didn't know how to pray, it seems that God in His never ending grace was still directing my paths, even when I had no definite plan. That is just how much God loves us. As for all those hours spent looking out into the ocean? Perhaps it wasn't just a waste of time after all.

For our light and momentary troubles are achieving for us an eternal glory that far outweighs them all. So we fix our eyes not on what is seen, but on what is unseen, since what is seen is temporary, but what is unseen is eternal. - 2 Corinthians 4:17-18

Before we continue let's let that last verse sink in a little. Read it again and digest it. Picture sitting on a boardwalk looking out over the ocean and just meditating for as long as it takes to empty your thoughts or lay all your burdens down. If you've never stared out into the vast blue sea then maybe you can substitute that vision with one where you are on top of a mountain looking out over a valley or a forest below. What do you see? Well if you are by the ocean you see a lot of salt water, sand, clouds, maybe even a few people. From the top of a mountain you might see a lot of trees, clouds, blue sky, birds, and maybe some towns in the distance. But don't fix your eyes on all that you see. Instead try *closing* your eyes. Now what do you see? According to Scripture it's what we *don't see* that we take with us through eternity. Does that make any sense to you? It's just one of those tiny verses in the Bible out of so many others that speak volumes and yet at the same some of us find it difficult to comprehend. Not being an ordained minister or even a theology student I don't pretend to know the exact meaning of this beautiful excerpt from one of the Apostle Paul's letters to the church in Corinth. But the next time you're in your happy place, whether it be the beach, the mountains, your favorite fishing hole, or even your own bedroom, close your eyes. *What do you see?* This might not be important to you at this moment in your life. But you might want to spend more time practicing silent prayer or meditation in your favorite sanctuary because the Bible says that eternity is filled with everything you don't see. We all need to wrap our heads around that. Perhaps five minutes a day in prayer with our eyes closed could change our lives. Can you 'will' different images or scenarios into existence when you close your eyes? If I were your football coach I might tell you to picture yourself making that big catch in the end zone. A basketball coach would tell his up-and-coming center to envision sinking the perfect three-pointer at the buzzer. And for some athletes that seems to work. How about you? When you close your eyes do you picture yourself doing great things, or does that only happen unconsciously while you are asleep? Everybody is different. Some people have a lot of vision. Take a really good architect for example. He or she might close their eyes and be able to create an entire masterpiece in their head given just a few minutes. Others might see nothing but a blank slate when their eyes are closed. It's okay. No two people are alike. If you are one of those who can't see anything with their eyes shut, don't despair. God gave us other senses and guess what? I could not find any passage in the Bible that says whatever you hear, smell, taste or touch does not follow you into eternity. What does that mean? I don't know for sure, and I might add that I am one of those who are wary of anyone who thinks they do know for sure what the afterlife will be like. All I know is the Bible only says that everything we see is temporary and everything we *don't* see is eternal. I've found nothing that says we can't hear music, taste and smell the rain, or feel the wind against our bodies when we get to Heaven. So who's to say that favorite song of yours cannot be heard after this life. If I close my eyes and play certain songs, I can dream that I am in

Heaven. I'm sure you have those songs too. On Carl Wilson's gravestone are the words "The heart and voice of an angel", and if I close my eyes and listen to the old song by the Beach Boys *"I Can Hear Music"* (Spector, Greenwich, Berry, 1966) I don't have to see anything but it feels like I am in Heaven listening to the angels sing. So what if you are one of those, like me, who don't visualize a whole lot with our eyes closed? How could we possibly know what Heaven is like if we can't visualize it? Well the truth is, and this is only my opinion of course, even the people who can picture an entire emerald city when they close their eyes have no idea what Heaven looks like because it looks like nothing we have ever seen before here on Earth. So don't think that because someone has the gift of visualizing skyscrapers or cars of the future or miracle cures to diseases that they have a clear picture of what the afterlife looks like; they don't have any more insight than you do. But if someone writes an untimely song that sounds like it could be sung by angels, well they might be onto something. Just remember that God's Word lasts forever and ever. Song lyrics I'm not so sure about. As far as food goes, we know that God fed manna to the Israelites while they wandered through the desert led by Moses in the Old Testament. One can only imagine how delicious food from Heaven must have tasted. All of this is merely food for thought so to speak. And those are all Heavenly thoughts. When one is trying to figure out a way to make more money to support his or her child(ren), one isn't usually thinking about what the afterlife is going to be like; there is only the here and now and the immediate future that is of major concern.

Obviously the next step would have to be to figure out a backup plan to replace radiography as a career. Yet nothing was coming to me. I would go to the beach almost daily and sit there waiting for an answer. After all, wasn't it God who had planted the idea of x-rays in my head five years before while I was still in the lawn business? Where was He now? I felt lost. I was not too savvy on Biblical passages but I did know a few basics like *Seek and You shall find. Ask and it will be given to you.* It wasn't as if I were unemployed; I still had my job at the hospital. But child support and the house I had moved into while still in the program cost more than the humble salary of a sterile prep tech back then. So it wasn't a matter of if I had to find another job; it was when and how long it would take to find one. Luckily I still had the second half of a school loan I had received for college during the previous semester, so I had a little breathing room. I could take the rest of summer trying to figure out what to do.

Around that time my ex-wife found out that I was out of school and asked if I wanted to spend more time with our daughter, who was 12 years old that summer. I thought that would be a great idea since we had not been able to spend much time together since before the x-ray program started the previous summer. Since I was still registered as a college student, all the various credit card companies were sending offers through the mail touting anywhere from $3000 to $5000 credit limits. I thought 'what the heck', I'd never had that much money at my fingertips in my whole life. Why not live a little? So I ordered a couple of credit cards and treated my daughter and myself like we were part of the royal family all summer long. That included the biggest and best theme parks in the state of Florida, renting cars for three-day

stays in motels, and lots of dinners and lunches at my
favorite restaurants on the beach. And then to top it off I
drove her up to North Georgia to visit my mom and step
dad in their home on top of a mountain. What a hoot that
was! To say that we all got to know each other a lot
better that week would be a huge understatement. The
stunts my daughter pulled on just that one trip assured
that it would be the last long vacation she and I would
ever take together. She was an absolute brat, and I so
badly wanted to just leave her at the McDonald's
somewhere in Georgia, where she got behind the wheel
of the rental car while I was throwing our trash into the
dumpster after lunch. By the time I had turned around to
head back to the vehicle, which was about thirty feet
away from the dumpster at the bottom of a 45° grade, she
had already put the car in Drive instead of Reverse, thank
God, and was headed up the hill toward me. Naturally I
began freaking out, and yelled at her to put the brakes on
so I could get into the car and take over. I don't know
how the situation didn't end up worse than it did, but I
am surely thankful that she didn't hurt or kill anyone.
When I finally got inside the car and got it down the hill

and back onto the parking lot, she calmly asked if I was mad at her. I was so mad I had to wait a few seconds before I could even answer without taking her head off.

"Mad?" I said. "Nooo I'm not mad. I'm just going to kill you!"

Her expression suddenly became serious. She knew I wasn't kidding. She could tell how mad I was. We both grew quiet and stayed that way for quite awhile. We had one more motel stay before home and I finally cooled off enough to engage in conversation with her. That wasn't even the worst stunt she pulled on me that summer but we both made it through, and I didn't even whoop her butt, much less kill her.

When we made it back home and I dropped her off at her mom's it was like a 50lb bag of fertilizer was just lifted off my shoulders. The past week with my daughter felt like it had lasted about a month. As with everything else there were two sides to the experience. Spiritually it had been good for our souls. We both had known we needed to spend some time together and learn more about each other, both the good and the bad. On the flip side, neither of us cared to see the other for quite some time. In fact one of us used to call the other at least once a week without fail, prior to our trip. Afterward we didn't speak to each other for about three months. When her mother called me up after the second month of our moratorium, she asked why I hadn't called in awhile. Still mad, I explained that I wasn't ready to talk to her yet, that she had misbehaved so badly. My ex said she had figured as much, and we left it at that.

But it's been said before, and there is some truth to the old saying that time heals all wounds. A few months later our relationship had healed itself through time, forgiveness, and understanding. And I suppose it did actually strengthen the father/daughter bond between us because she found out what she needed to know, I guess; that she could push me as far as I could stand it and I still wouldn't lay a hand on her. Why should I have? I hadn't been around all the time to discipline her the way I would have liked, so how could I have expected her to respect me 100%? As for my part, I learned that my daughter was growing up with some qualities I did not like, that I did not recognize as coming from me or anyone in my immediate family. If I had ever disrespected my parents to that extent, my dad would have never let me leave my room. But it was what it was. She was 12 years old with a mind of her own and was already showing the full stubbornness that has always been one of our family traits. In those terms she did remind me a lot of myself.

So the summer of '95, though far from going the way I had planned, turned out to be just the way God had planned it all along. I needed to get to know my daughter before she was all grown up and she needed to spend some time with her dad. Times like those are priceless and one doesn't appreciate them until much later in life. Only now as I write this 25 years later do I realize that, had I still been in the x-ray program that summer instead of spending all that time with my daughter as she was entering the awkward experience we call puberty, I may have missed the opportunity to learn more about her, both the good and the bad. And after all these years it makes me smile, because it is a reminder that I never asked God for direction back then. I just set my mind on that one big goal, put all my eggs into one basket, and gave it everything I had. And He came through, not by letting me succeed in that one goal of becoming an x-ray tech, but to show me what was more important: a relationship with my only biological child.

God always directs our paths. No one achieves anything worthwhile without God's direction. It wasn't until I became familiar with His nature that I realized what I had been doing wrong for the majority of my life. You see, whenever I set my sights on a goal I would go after it, oftentimes relentlessly and at the cost of spending time with family and friends. And more often than not I would fall short of my goals for one reason or another. So what had I been doing wrong? The answer is really quite simple and can be summed up in just one short sentence taken from Scripture:

But seek ye first the kingdom of God, and His righteousness;

and all these shall be added unto you. - Matthew 6:33

It goes on to say that if you follow that simple instruction, everything else will fall into place. So the next time you get a wild hair (and I've had my share) and decide on a new career, a new invention, a new hobby that might take up all your spare time, or even a new car, you would do well to remember that.

Seek **first** *the* *kingdom* *of* *God...*

9 REGRESSING OR DIGRESSING?

Merriam-Webster, one of the most trusted names in American dictionaries since the 1800's defines the word *regress* as follows:

- an act or the privilege of going or coming back;
- movement backward to a previous and especially worse or more primitive state or condition;
- the act of reasoning backward.

Not to be confused with the similar word *digress* which, according to Merriam-Webster once again, is described as:

"to turn aside especially from the main subject of attention or course of argument."

The definition of *regress* doesn't need much clarification; it is clearly an act of going backward, whether referring to an unintended career change or a deterioration of mental or physical health. The word *digress* however, has quite a few synonyms and as such needs to be understood in context, depending on the subject being discussed. Most commonly it is used when discussing a *deviation* or change of a chosen path. Another common synonym of *digress* is the word *swerve* as in *swerved* to avoid hitting a dog.

Why the grammar lesson on the two words *regress* and *digress*? Well, besides the fact that this chapter's whole focus hinges on the difference between definitions of the two words, it is important to know what each one means in order to clarify the story. As you will see, the two words may be confused at times in daily usage because of their similarities, but there is a great difference in their two meanings when used to describe someone's choice when their life meets a crossroads.

And that is precisely what this chapter is all about. The previous chapter illustrated the height of disappointment and the uncertainty and despair it can bring about in one's future. Now we will find out the consequences one faces when he or she chooses to deviate from their chosen path, either by regressing or digressing.

Despite all the soul searching, all the hours upon hours of solitude spent meditating on the waves at the beach, I never really came up with an acceptable alternative to the radiography program as a prosperous and interesting career choice. I worked at a picture framing warehouse for the time being because one thing I knew for sure was that I needed the money. Working in the Sterile Prep department at the hospital wasn't going to pay the bills without a part-time job. So I worked in a warehouse punching picture frames together, all the while checking the newspaper ads for other jobs. Along with a house payment and the other usual bills that are the norm for everyone living on their own, i.e., utilities, auto insurance, homeowner's insurance, etc., I also had accumulated over $5000 in credit card debt after a summer full of spending sprees with my daughter. At

20%+ interest rates, it was clear that whatever job I could find had better pay pretty well lest I should be working for nothing, just 'spinning my wheels' as my old boss used to call it.

The dilemma was a familiar one, experienced by virtually everyone who has ever had to search for a new job on the fly. In your heart you really want to land that dream job doing what you would love to be doing for a living. Then the reality hits home that you either need experience or more schooling to qualify for that job, so you have to settle for something you already know. I was 37 years old with beaucoup experience in golf course maintenance and a few years of lawn maintenance under my belt. Much as I would have loved to spread my wings again and learn a new trade like civil engineering, auto mechanics, or teaching history, there was no way I was going back to school right away after spending the last three years hitting the books and doing clinical rotations all for naught. No way. Nor did I really care to work at another golf course after working at the same course for ten years and getting absolutely nowhere while spending hours upon hours driving tractors and fancy turf mowing machines. So I guess you can surmise what kind of job I ended up with.

Working for my football coach boss in the lawn business for two years full-time and later on two more years part-time might not have made me much smarter, but it did teach me a lot about discipline and hard work. I had always thought that I was a disciplined hard worker before, until I started working for the coach. He taught me what discipline and hard work were all about. By the time he was through with me I just knew that no matter what I did after leaving that job, nobody could accuse me of being a slacker. I could work alongside the best of 'em. Guess it's no small wonder I finally found a job working for an enterprising entrepreneur who took the business of lawn maintenance to a new level I had never seen before or since. He had around twenty guys on the payroll and split them up into seven crews that were assigned their own properties to take care of each week. How he did it was pure genius and it seemed like we always pulled off each day's work without a single hitch. I'm not even going to attempt to remember how many properties we maintained, including small villages, community entrances, beach mansions, and everything in between. I will say that the work we did each week as a whole dwarfed that of what we did when I was working for the coach, just as it should have. This new crew I was working with had seven times the amount of guys. And just like working for the coach, everyone had to pull their weight. As a rule, lawn maintenance is mostly routine work, not too exciting or eventful. But I'm telling you, when you've got twenty guys working together as a team with one goal, and that is to finish the designated properties of each day, it's a beautiful thing. Anytime one of the seven mini-crews ran into a snag that slowed them down, another crew would finish their job early and head over to that crew's jobsite to help them finish on time. In some very rare cases all seven crews would end up coming to the aid of a single crew that ran into some bad luck that day, resulting in twenty guys buzzing around a property or village like a swarm of bees on a honeycomb.

As for reflecting on what life was like working at the large lawn care company, it was a lot of hard work, but not quite as hard as working for the coach. The reasons were two-fold: 1) There were so many other guys working together, I never once felt overwhelmed by the amount of work to be done each week, and (2) The coach knew about riding mowers and velky attachments for 36" mowers, he just didn't believe in using them. I think he was all about strength and fitness and how their benefits could best be derived from working in the yards every day. The entrepreneur was more about providing the best equipment available for his workers and keeping it running in tip-top condition. In essence, working for the entrepreneur was a lot like being a kid in a candy store for a lawn mowing enthusiast. The equipment was second only to that of a high class golf course maintenance department. The mowers very rarely broke down and if they did, either the boss or his mechanic would have another mower out to the jobsite within a half hour. Like I said, it was a very smooth operation. And that's all I have to say about it really. For three full years my life revolved around showing up for work at 7:00 every morning Monday through Friday and either mowing, trimming, weedeating, planting, mulching, digging, or a combination of all of the above; then clocking out at 3:00 and getting home by 3:30 with just enough time to take a shower and get ready for work at the hospital, where I pulled 40 hours a week working Monday through Saturday. I still made time to see my daughter every other Sunday but other than that I guess you could say I had no life. Good thing I wasn't married back then. Who could expect a wife to stay home with a guy who was only home on Sundays? A friend of mine whom I met in the x-ray department while doing clinicals once accused me of being an "indentured servant". Ha! I can laugh about it now, but it sure did ring true back then. Anyway, after my three-year term of indenture (haha) was up I decided to leave the lawn business once again and take the summer of 1999 off, still working at the hospital of course. I had found a girlfriend the previous winter and it gave us a little more time to spend together over the summer. By the end of August I had found another job, after having cashed out an annuity of over $1000.00 to get through my hiatus. Facing the usual dilemma of experience vs. unattainable dream job, I found work at another golf course by the famous Indian River Lagoon. It was comforting somehow knowing that in a pinch I could count on my experience on the golf course to find a job doing something I actually enjoyed to some degree.

It had been eleven years since I worked at the other golf course. The courses differed in many ways but I was a different person as well. During those eleven years I had worked for two vastly different lawn services, gone back to school to study math, English, science, and history for the first time since high school in 1976, and got accepted into and then dropped out of an x-ray program at the community college. I had watched my daughter grow up from a 5 year-old sweetheart into a 16 year-old parents' nightmare. And I myself had grown from a beach bum into a middle-aged man who at the age of 41 was more than satisfied to just be able to work two full-time jobs in order to pay child support, put food in my stomach and a roof over my head that I could call my own. The biggest mistake I had made thus far? Well except for not praying enough and learning about God and Jesus, probably buying what could have been called a car of my dreams: a 1996 Pontiac Grand Am Special Edition, shiny black with red pin-striping down the sides. It was sweet, no question about that; but to the tune of

$12,000.00 at $300.00 a month for six years? I really should have known better.

Anyway, the golf course job fit right in with my hospital schedule, and I got right back into the routine of working all day long from Mondays through Saturdays, just as I had done in the lawn business for the previous three years. It was definitely easier work than either of my former lawn crews, just as I knew it would be. Golf course work, as I have already stated in both this book and one of my others, **"Mowing at the Master's Level"** (Amazon 2017), consists of about 80% riding on turf mowers all day and maybe 20% manual labor, unless you happen to be the irrigation specialist on the crew. That can be a challenging job at times, especially when there is a large blowout in a mainline pipe. There were few surprises when I took on the position of greenskeeper at the golf course in '99. I said the courses were different. Some major differences that come to mind are: very few trees in the roughs compared to my first course; nowhere to just sit on your machine and chill for a spell during the hot summer months. The superintendent, like the residents, were not cool at all at my new course. Another difference was the greens mowing method. I have mentioned before and gone into great detail in my **Mowing...** book how fun it had been to mow greens with walk-behind reel-type mowers when I was a young man. It was great exercise and a refreshing spiritual experience as well. My new golf course supervisor didn't believe wholeheartedly in the walk-behind mower concept. As a result, he did not even have a walk-behind mowing program until about a year after I started working there. He liked the job that a triplex mower performed. The triplex had three wheels and three mowing reels and was a riding mower. To me, a walk-behind mower will always do a better job, and if I ever have to work at another golf course I will make sure they hand-mow their greens before I even consider working on a course, no matter how beautiful the course may be. Anyway, those were the major differences that come to mind between the two courses I worked on eleven years apart.

The job at my new course only lasted about a year and a half, for reasons you will find out in the next chapter, but the question remains: Were the two job choices following my exit from the radiography program a *regression* or *digression*? I ask myself that question sometimes when I reflect back on the past and occasionally it haunts me; not terribly, how you might read somewhere in a mystery novel, *"He was haunted by the past."* I've just had a few *If only* moments about that particular period in my life. I mean, if you go all the way back to what my life was like before I even started working at the hospital, I was living on the beach, mowing grass for a living. It was a simple life, probably healthy to some degree, except for the inherent danger of skin cancer, which could have been avoided with the proper protection. At first glance it would appear that following the x-ray program, I *regressed* or *moved backward* to a previous and more primitive state or condition. You can see why sometimes in reflection I simply resign myself to the conclusion that I went through a serious *regression* after dropping out of the program. And yet the positive side of my conscience, the one that always finds the good in everything, reminds me that by working for one of the largest lawn companies in the business and later finding work at another golf course, I not only expanded my horizons, but took my knowledge and skills in golf course and lawn maintenance to a new level. Now you might be saying *"Pfffft. Well whoop de do"* to that last statement, but if in this life you attain a status in *any* career, whether it be in engineering or as a sous chef, that gives you the confidence to say to the hiring manager or supervisor of any job in that career, "I *know* I can do this job and you *won't* be disappointed if you hire me," well then you have accomplished something my friend. And it is exactly to that end that I have concluded, with the help of the good part of my conscience, that my move when I reached one of the biggest forks in the road back in 1995 was a *digression.* Rather than moving backward, I merely *deviated* or changed my chosen path. And of course, since God was directing my paths the whole way, everything turned out fine, just as He had always planned it.

> *Trust in the Lord with all your heart*
> *and lean not on your own understanding.*
> Proverbs3:5(NIV)

10 REBUILDING WITH DIESEL, AND A REVELATION

After five years of working two full-time jobs with little to no free time to myself, I was long overdue for some kind of change. Again I went to the Help Wanted ads in the local paper to see what was out there. And again, just as it was the last time I had searched for a better job, there was nothing new under the sun. By the end of Y2K I had been working in Sterile Processing for ten years. Looking back now, that wasn't nearly as long as it seemed to be at the time. I was hoping to find something to fill that time slot in the evenings from 3:00 to 11:00 so that I could quit my job at the hospital, work at the golf course during the day and somewhere else in the afternoons/evenings. Yet I didn't want to work in another kitchen. Talk about regressing! Going back to washing dishes, pots and pans, and everything else for just over minimum wage would have been a move only out of sheer desperation, and thankfully I wasn't there yet. But boy was I ready for a change!

One evening in early January of 2001, while relaxing by the fireplace in front of the TV after another long 16-hour workday, an ad on a local Classified Ads channel caught my eye. Against a deep blue background, in black letters it said that a local truck stop was looking to hire diesel mechanics *with no previous experience needed.* They would train. Couldn't believe my eyes. I had always wanted to be a mechanic but couldn't afford to pay for training. And here was an opportunity to learn how to work on diesel engines while earning a paycheck. So excited I didn't even think to get a pen and paper to write down the phone number. Stayed glued in front of the TV set until the ad came around again about a half hour later. Turns out they didn't even have a phone number listed on the ad. One was supposed to apply in person at the listed address, which I recognized as the main truck stop in my hometown. This all sounded too good to be true, but hey I had nothing to lose so it was worth a shot to drive a few miles up the highway to see if it was for real or if the ad was even still valid.

So the next morning, a Saturday, I drove to the truck stop, parked in front by the restaurant, and walked around back to where the two huge mechanic bays stood amidst a large convoy of parked tractor trailers of all colors, sizes, and shapes. I'd never been that close to so many big rigs in my life. If it weren't for the sheer excitement of anticipating the opportunity to learn how to work on them, it would have been an intimidating moment for sure. There was a small trucker's parts store beside the two large bays where I assumed the manager's office would be. I walked right into that store and asked the young man behind the counter if they were still looking for diesel mechanics. He looked up at me, probably noticed that I was around 40 years-old, and said,

"Do you have experience?"

Now normally I would have gotten discouraged just by the asking of that question, but I had a gut feeling that I was going to get this job, so I didn't even flinch.

"No, but I caught your ad on TV and it said they would train."

The young man looked at me with sort of a puzzled look on his face and said,

"Well why do you want to be a diesel mechanic?" It was an innocent question, and I am quite sure he asked it because well, why would a man heading into middle-age with no experience in diesel mechanics even think about the idea of working on big rigs? But I had an answer for him that he seemed to be okay with right out of the gate.

"My dad was a mechanic."

The young man nodded and showed me to the manager's office. Turned out his dad was the owner of the business. He understood what it was like to want to follow in one's father's footsteps. When I spoke with the manager in his office he asked me the exact same question and I gave him the exact same answer. Thus began my next phase of life as a diesel mechanic, doing what I had always wanted to do since visiting the garage where my Dad worked back in Toronto when I was a child of perhaps six or seven. I loved everything about it;

the smells of hand cleaner, grease, burning metal, rubber tires, and body putty; and the sounds of air tools screaming in the air, grinders grinding down sharp metal edges and the sound of a welding machine's buzz while the welder joins two pieces of metal together.

There was nothing else I would have rather done than someday become an auto mechanic just like Dad. He was my childhood hero. In my eyes he could always fix anything. So when he first asked me at a really young age, I forget how old I was, what I thought I might want to be when I grew up, I said without hesitation an auto mechanic. But my dad was different than most. Instead of being the proud father, happy that his son wanted to follow in his footsteps, he always tried to talk both my brother and me out of becoming mechanics. He said the work was too dangerous for the small paycheck one could expect to make. I was persistent until that day he sat me down on the patio of our home when I was a young teenager and told me it was about time to think about what I wanted to do for a living. By then he had totally talked me out of ever being a mechanic, so I just told him that all I wanted to do was race motocross, to which he just shook his head. All the while I thought to myself, *Well if you wouldn't have talked me out of it, I would have been working on cars by now.*

So that's the story of why I had always wanted to be a mechanic but never once applied for even an entry level position. Fast forward about 30 years and I guess that desire to be just like my dad one day never really went away; it was only hibernating, waiting for the right time; God's time. Thirty years is quite a long time in human terms, I mean depending upon how old you are, you might say 30 years is a *very* long time to wait for something. I remember someone telling me once, when I was about 21, that if you want to ever really be something one day you have to work at it for ten years before your dream comes to its fruition. And I thought wow, that would take a lot of dedication. But it took 30 years for one of my childhood dreams to come true, and I hadn't even dedicated my life to it. It came only by the grace of God. And now, not only was I going to have the opportunity to be a mechanic, I would be working on big rigs with huge diesel engines, which are inherently much safer than working with gasoline engines, in terms of the fact that gas is flammable and diesel is combustible. But that is probably the only reason anyone would consider that working on diesel engines is safer than gas engines. Everything on a big rig is 10 times heavier than anything on an automobile. Drop a car tire on your foot and you might hurt your toes. Drop a truck tire on your foot and it could easily break your foot.

I'll tell you what though, when I got that job at the truck stop I knew for the first without a doubt that God was directing my path, even if I didn't think he had been directing it before. That knowledge would be confirmed about a week and a half into the new job. You see, after the first week of working at the golf course every morning Monday through Friday from 6:30 to 3:00 in the afternoons, and going to work at the truck stop from 4:00 to 11:00pm or later if I was still working on a truck, I began to re-think my situation. Had I really done the right thing? The idea that I could work both jobs looked and sounded good in theory. I had been working two full-time jobs for five years, since 1996. But the hospital had always been my evening job, and it wasn't terribly hard work, although decontam could be challenging on occasion. This new setup was pretty crazy to be sure; working outdoors all morning and into the afternoon, only to spend the evenings working on tractor-trailers. I was beginning to think my enthusiasm for finally getting to be a mechanic was premature, to put it nicely. And it was still only February. What would happen in summer, when the Florida sun saps all the energy out of the body and soul, and leaves you with only the desire to go home and take a nap each day after work? I was pretty sure I would have to think of a better idea. But I should have known better by then. After all, God had given me plenty of signs that He was directing my paths; surely he wouldn't forsake me now. Sure enough He showed me a better way, a way that would make the situation do-able and still allow me to realize my dream of becoming a diesel mechanic.

It was during the second week of working the new golf course maintenance/diesel mechanic routine. I was on the triplex mowing greens, a great time to do a little critical thinking. After all, I had been mowing grass almost non-stop for over twenty years at that point, and had done a lot of thinking and planning while on the job.

Not only that, but the triplex had always been one of my favorite machines. Basically the operator would drive down the fairway to a green or a tee, pull up onto the edge and drop all three reels at the same time by simply putting pressure on a foot pedal on the floorboard. Then it was a matter of going back and forth on the green or tee, making sure to keep the lines perfectly straight and lift/drop the reels at exactly the proper time so as to not burn any edges. Anyway, I was on the 8th green when the gears in my brain really began to turn in sync. The question was how could I sustain these two jobs? I had desired nothing more than to leave the hospital after ten years in sterile processing, a job I had taken in order to get me through the x-ray program. With that dream shattered, I had seen no other reason to stay at the hospital. I figured if I could keep two jobs that I enjoyed, life would be a whole lot better. But I obviously never thought the whole thing through. It was like jumping out of the frying pan and into the fire. I would have given anything at that moment to get my old job back in sterile prep. Yet I still wanted to be a diesel mechanic. What to do? There was no way to work the day shift at either job;

those positions were sealed up by workers who had claimed that cherished shift for many years and would never give them up. Distraught by the seemingly unchangeable situation, I kept on mowing straight lines on the 8th green until….. BAM! With only a couple more passes left on the green, my mind jumped to something our new OR manager had said during her first meeting with the sterile prep team about two months before. She said that she was always open to new suggestions, and even mentioned the possibility of hiring someone to work three 12-hour shifts on Fridays, Saturdays, and Sundays. BINGO! It was a revelation from none other than the King of Kings, the Lord of Lords, God Almighty. All I would have to do was find out if my former supervisor at the hospital would hire me back for the weekend shift, and if she would, then ask the shop manager at the truck stop if I could work Mondays through Thursdays 32 hours/week instead of a full 40 hour week. I knew for sure that it was meant to be when both bosses agreed to the new hours. I was ecstatic. Staying home all morning or getting to ride my bike whenever I wanted to until 2:00 or so felt almost as good as working only part-time.

Sure, I had to work all weekend at the hospital from Friday through Sunday night, but it kept me out of trouble and I still needed to try to save money. After all, my daughter would turn 18 during that same year (2001), and I wanted to be able to scale back to only one job shortly after child support payments were finished. My credit card debt was still high, along with that $300.00/month payment for the Grand Am. I figured on being debt-free in about five more years, if I could just stay working both jobs a little longer.

I wore my blue mechanic's uniform proudly, even though they all had grease stains that could never be washed out. Working on big rigs was filthy dirty work. I'd been used to getting dirty every day working in dusty yards, but dust was nowhere near as dirty as tractor-trailer grease. Since I had no previous experience as a mechanic I took most of the grease jobs, or "PM Specials" that came into the bay. For that dubious honor I would first guide the truck driver over the grease pit, which was exactly what it sounds like, a roughly 25-foot long by 5-foot wide by 6-foot deep concrete pit in one of the two large truck bays, a designated area for grease jobs, clutch adjustments, oil changes, and whatever other jobs that could be performed easier while standing under the tractor or trailer. The *PM Special* had around 100 point-checks, which meant that there were at least 100 items that needed to be checked and serviced, if needed, on each rig that parked over the pit. For the first four months or so, I can't remember how long exactly, that pit, along with the rest of the floors in both bays, were so filthy nasty with grease, I didn't think they had ever cleaned the place, I mean *ever*. Then my shop manager left and found a job with another truck stop in his hometown, and they hired a new manager. He made it a priority to clean the shop with a steam genie, squeegees, and a 3-foot wide push broom. We worked on that floor for a week or better until the shop looked like new. It was no small feat. The contrast was nothing short of amazing. I don't know how the other mechanics felt about it but it made me more proud to work there, and less self-conscious about being a 'grease monkey.' In time the cleanings would lapse in frequency a little but the shop was never again as black and greasy as it had been when I first started working there.

Working at the truck stop was challenging and there were plenty of evenings I felt like throwing in the towel, but all the hard work I had done in the past, along with the desire to fulfill my dad's legacy for however long I could take it, allowed me to persevere through every shift I worked there. One thing I was really proud of was that after a few successful welding jobs on some trucks and trailers, I became the main arc welder on our shift. The kicker was that the only experience I had was welding broken motorcycle frames, exhaust pipes, etc. with a 50-amp welder Dad had bought me when I was something like 16 years old. That brings me to another reason I was glad I took that giant leap of faith to become a diesel mechanic. I would go over to visit my dad about once a week to talk shop with him, the first time in my life I had ever been able to do that. I would tell him about a tire that had exploded while I was airing it up in the cage, or a weld job I did that I was super proud of, or anything new I might have learned that week that made me feel more like a mechanic and not just a grease monkey. It was so awesome to have been able to share those experiences with my dad, and in return he would share some of his own from when he had been a mechanic back in Toronto. He once told me that I was starting to be a mechanic at the age most guys usually quit and find a different line of work. But that didn't phase me. I wasn't going to quit until either I was good and ready or God told me to quit.

I could likely go on for hours about some of the unique challenges and jobs I experienced while at the truck stop. Most if not all of my other careers have been pretty routine; working on big rigs was anything but that. No two tractor-trailers were exactly alike and each one presented different challenges. You could certainly say that I never regretted for one minute my decision to try my hand at diesel mechanics. The skills picked up at the truck stop have helped me get through my own mechanical issues since then, both on my vehicles and in the home. And the tools! I started out with a small toolbox, Craftsman I think, that I had used on my motorcycles, all the way back to 1980. I now have two full 2-tier tool chests (say that fast three times), one of them full of my dad's old tools, some of them dating back to the 1950's. Do I still need all these tools?

Probably not, but you know how it is; as soon as you get rid of something, that's when you will need it.

Rather than ramble on about trucks or truckers or how cool it was to work on Caterpillar engines, I'll just name five memorable incidents that come to mind whenever I think about my years at the truck stop. Here goes:

1) There was my very first night on the job, when a car hauler (a tractor-trailer pulling cars, or a 'parking lot', whatever you want to call it) pulled into the bay with a full load of cars on the back, about a dozen of them, and needed someone to change a tire on the trailer. I was standing in the bay waiting for another mechanic to show up so I could see how he would get under the back of the trailer. There didn't seem to me like there was enough space between the hauler's frame and the ground to crawl under and jack up the rear wheel. Both of the other mechanics were busy so the truck driver parked the trailer in the bay and went into the restaurant to grab a bite to eat, like they usually did. A few minutes later the shop supervisor walked up to me and said,

"Okay Richard, ready for your first truck?"

Long story short, a car hauler holding twelve brand new cars was my first job at the truck stop. How difficult was it to get a jack underneath the trailer of a car hauler? I once received a $20.00 tip for staying past midnight just to change a tire on a 'parking lot' full of cars. It wasn't easy. There I was, first time jacking up a tractor-trailer rig, and I couldn't even figure out how I was supposed to get under the trailer or where to put the jack. Luckily my supervisor wasn't all that cold hearted, and he guided me through the steps on that first truck. After that I never had a problem getting under another trailer. The biggest problem usually came about when the lug nuts on a rusted out wheel were frozen to the lugs and couldn't be jarred loose, even with the huge air hammer guns we used to loosen the lug nuts.

2) After my probationary period of three months, I felt really comfortable doing PM's, oil changes, and grease jobs. It was time to start learning new skills on the trucks. Belt jobs, i.e., alternator, a/c, and fan belt replacements, were fairly simple tasks, or so the other mechanics would tell me. I had changed several belts on

my own vehicles in the past, probably at least one belt change for each car or van I had ever owned. It wasn't too difficult. How difficult could it be on a Caterpillar, Detroit diesel, or Cummins engine? So I took on a belt job one night on a Cummins engine, not the most popular engine in trucking, at least down here in Florida. I figured I would have to loosen the alternator bolt first and then the belt would slip right off. Opened up the hood and found that there were actually two belts. *Oh brother, don't tell me I've got to take the fan off or something like that.* I didn't think I was up to such a complex operation yet. So about an hour into the job, I've still only got one belt off, the water pump is loosened, and I've all but got the fan bolts removed from the water pump when one of the other mechanics came over and asked what I was trying to do. I told him I was changing out the belts. He gave me that look, like 'What a rookie!' and said,

"Man, that's a 15-minute job on a Cummins!"

I just looked at him like he had ruined my whole night. He went to his tool chest, grabbed a wrench, and used it to activate a spring-loaded lever that held the water pump belt tight against the pulleys. I stood there half in awe, the other half in anger. I made it a point thereafter to try to find out somehow if there is ever an easier way to do any job. Sometimes the diesel engineers have already made the job easier for the mechanic before the engine even makes it into the truck.

3) Road calls were standard issue at the truck stop. Anytime a trucker called the shop to report a breakdown out on the road, within 50 miles in either direction, we were expected to respond. This responsibility was shared equally among the mechanics as much as possible. The perk was that road calls paid about double the amount of a regular job done in the shop. There was actually an even better perk than that. The clock started when the mechanic left the shop in the service truck and ended when he pulled back in. So if a trucker was broken down an hour's drive away and the job took an hour to complete, *cha-ching!* You got paid for three hours of work. And to be fair, the supervisor would normally only send a mechanic out on a service call if he knew that he could do the job without much trouble. In other words, he would not have sent me out to the middle of nowhere to

fix a truck with locked up trailer brakes because brakes were definitely not my specialty. In fact, if I had any specialties at all they would have been tires and oil changes. After only a year I could change tires and do PM's with the best of them. I've taken a few good road calls in my day and made some fun easy money, at least as far as mechanic's jobs go. I've changed trailer tires on the side of the interstate, changed an alternator belt or two out on the highway; heck, one time I got to take five gallons of diesel out to a truck that was about an hour's drive out into the Florida boonies, which was usually anywhere west on Route #60. I was pretty good at getting trucks re-started following an oil and filter change, so the supervisor was pretty confident I would have no problem. Got out there and the truck driver was so glad to see me I felt like a hero. I dumped the fuel in his tank, primed the fuel lines and that big old diesel fired right up. That was probably my all-time favorite job because I had been stressing on the drive out that the truck might need something more than just fuel. Then what would I have done? But I was blessed that day. All in all I'd say my road calls were pretty successful. But, as my brother always said when we were growing up, *"There's always one."* That was short for *"There's always one person, one thing, or one bad situation that ruins the whole experience."* For me that 'one' was the time I got sent out on a road call in the dark of night to fix a flat on the right front tire of a Greyhound bus. I knew I was in trouble when I pulled up to the bus and saw it leaning so far over on the front right corner that the bumper was almost touching the ground. The passengers were all cheering when I pulled up, so I might have felt like an even greater hero on this road call if I thought I could have fixed it. But I just couldn't see how I would be able to get a jack under the chassis to lift the wheel up off the ground. The driver asked if I thought it might be helpful if he could lighten the load. I shrugged my shoulders and said it would be worth a try, so he asked all the passengers to exit out of the front of the bus. Even though it was a major inconvenience, they were still so appreciative that I had shown up, they were all thanking and blessing me before I even started the job. But it didn't help much at all. After trying to squeeze the jack under the front bumper from every angle, I decided to radio the shop for help. The assistant shop supervisor arrived in about a half-hour and together we finished the job. I was so grateful he showed up. We had had our differences in the past but after the bus incident I never said anything bad about him ever again. It really sucks when the 'hero' rescuer arrives on the scene and finds out he's going to need to be rescued himself. But it happens. Whatever it takes to get the truck (or bus, or whatever) back on the road.

4) I couldn't keep listing all the unfortunate jobs I did as a diesel mechanic without mentioning at least one job that made it all worthwhile. One evening we were a little slow, the other mechanics were busy, and there were no trucks over the oil pit. I was kind of standing around trying to look busy when a big Peterbilt pulled into the bay. The driver shut 'er down, got out of the cab and walked purposefully to the front center of the truck. Some of the drivers liked to raise their own hoods. I was never sure if it was meant to be some kind of a sign or if they just wanted to help out somehow. Anyway, this guy was one of them. Now Peterbilts, as a rule, always had the largest hoods in the industry, second to none. And

more often than not they would have the engine to go with it. In that sense, this was your typical Peterbilt or 'Pete.' The driver popped the latches on either side, tilted that big hood up on its hinges, and let me tell you what! Inside was the biggest Caterpillar diesel I had ever seen come into the bays at the truck stop. I can't remember which model it was or how many cylinders, but it was bigger than any Detroit or Cummins I had ever seen by far. I found myself actually wishing he would have pulled it into the other bay, over the grease pit, so I could give that big dog a PM Special. You know, bragging rights and all that. The driver strolled over to the accessory shop to put in a service order. I walked around for a few more minutes; still no trucks rolling in over the pit. Then the door of our parts room swung open and my supervisor walked out just as the driver walked over from the front of the accessory shop. The supervisor called me over to where they were standing by the monster Caterpillar engine, so I joined them with what must have been an eager yet cautious look on my face. The shop boss, a big guy who looked a little roly-poly but could move pretty well and knew his way around a big rig, stood there, hands on his hips, and said to me,

"Ever change out a thermostat on one of these things?"

I thought for a second then said,

"No, but I've changed quite a few on my own vehicles."

The driver chuckled. To a trucker, you haven't changed anything and you haven't fixed anything until you've done it on a big rig. But my boss didn't change his serious expression. He just looked at me in the eyes and said,

"Well this engine's got two of 'em. You got two hours. Better get busy. I'll take you through the first one and you can do the second one on your own."

All I could think was *Wow!* There was no time to be scared or even a little intimidated by the job. I grabbed my favorite ratchet and some sockets and went to work. The driver was pretty concerned when I had only changed out the first thermostat in two hours, and began complaining to my boss, but the boss man told him not to worry about it, he would comp the extra time it took. One thing I had learned by that time, before the monster Caterpillar driver had even pulled into the bay with his huge Peterbilt, was that drivers with Cat engines under their hoods were the most difficult to please. They didn't want a mechanic to work on their Cat; they wanted an engineer. Actually, I think they would have much preferred to bring every little problem, every little idiosyncrasy with their engines, back to the Caterpillar factory in Illinois for fine tuning. It pained them so to let a mere truck stop diesel mechanic get his grubby little handprints all over their shiny yellow paint.

I performed enough oil changes, coolant replacements, and filter changes on Caterpillar engines to grow weary of their owners coming out to the shop to critique every single step of the process. It is only after all these years away from the job that I finally understand what all the fuss was about. Simply put, Cat engines are the Ferrari of diesel engines; but more than that, they are the American workhorse version of a Ferrari engine. Everything about working on a Caterpillar engine was more difficult than any Detroit or Cummins. The tolerances were closer, the bolts were tighter; I once

broke a brand new Mac Tools 24" breaker bar on a
Caterpillar oil plug, trying to drop the oil into the sump
pan. But whenever you've finished a job on that big
engine and the driver turns the key to crank it up, there's
not a better feeling as a mechanic when she starts purring
like a big Cat, especially if there are absolutely no leaks.
That means you did your job and are worthy in the eyes
of at least one Caterpillar owner/operator. He just might
ask for you to work on his truck the next time he comes
into the shop.

So that was one of my best experiences working as a
mechanic. There were others as well, but I gained a lot of
respect from the other mechanics and for myself as well.
And of course I got to tell my dad all about the
thermostat job on the huge Cat.

5) The last of the top five memorable experiences
from the truck stop was a day I will never forget. Nor
will any other American who was at least five years old
on that day during the first of my 2-year occupation at the
truck stop. The year was 2001, the month of September.
Eight months into my new career as a diesel mechanic,
the truck stop had been so busy servicing trucks, the

supervisor had hired two more mechanics for the evening shift, for a total of four of us. We never lacked for business and all of us were clocked in on jobs for most of the shift; very important since the majority of our pay was on a commission basis. There were only a couple of jobs that paid a flat rate: changing tires and PM Specials. Both of those soon became my bread and butter. We had been so busy of late that I had recently invested in a slightly used MAC tool chest about as tall as me, and a bunch of new tools. I planned on staying a while, at least for a couple of years, in order to obtain my ASE certification. But then came that awful day, September 11th.

I rolled out of bed around 9:00 that morning after a late night at the truck stop. Then, per usual routine, I pushed the start button on my fairly new e-machine dinosaur computer sitting on the desk beside my bed. Next of course was to head to the kitchen, start a pot of coffee, and throw something together for breakfast, most likely just a bowl of cereal. After breakfast and a cup of joe I headed back into the bedroom to check the computer and see if anything was going on in the world.

Those old computers, when hooked up to the telephone lines, were really slow to start up, nothing like the speed they are now. I used it mostly to check the weather, the surf report, and whatever else caught my eye as I surfed the web. It was a new technology for me and I was having fun with it. I remember MSN was my home page. As I fiddled with my mouse, the blank screen finally began to come back to life. And there at the top of the screen was an image I had never seen before, and it took a minute to figure out what was going on. I mean, this couldn't really be happening. The most bizarre thing that had ever happened in my lifetime up to that point had been man landing on the moon. But there on the screen was what appeared to be the World Trade Center in New York with one of the towers billowing thick black smoke from what looked like the top ten floors or better. It was all so surreal. Was this someone's idea of a sick joke? After a minute or so of watching that scene unfold on the computer screen, it finally hit me that if this were real it would be on the national news. There was a 19" TV on the dresser beside my desk, so I turned it on and immediately realized this was no joke. It was breaking news and it was on every major network. So it was still before 10:00, one of the towers was burning like crazy, and the news reporters were acting pretty nonchalant like oh, this is a big deal but it could have been a lot worse. I had no clue as to how they were planning to put out the fire but only assumed the FDNY already had it under control. No one seemed to be panicking about it. What about the people working on the top floors? Did they all get out? The cameras weren't zooming in on any jumpers, only showing the view from another tall building about a mile away. It seemed like they were never going to say what had happened or how, until finally one of the reporters, presumably the anchor, said that a large airplane had accidentally clipped the top of the building while flying low over NYC. Whaaaat? Sounded a little far-fetched but if they were okay with it, who was I to question the absurdity of it all? Then, moments later something even stranger happened , this time on national television, that defied all probability except for only one explanation. A second airplane, clearly a large jumbo jet airliner like a 747, rammed right into the other tower at the same height, as if trying to fly straight through it. Like the vast majority of Americans, all I could do was sit there with my eyes wide open and say,

"Oh my God."

The rest of the story is now written in the annals of American history under the heading of 'America's Worst Tragedies.' There were reporters broadcasting from buildings close enough to ground zero that you could hear the bodies landing on cars parked outside from over 1500 feet above; smoke billowing out of both skyscrapers like two massive chimneys side by side; firefighters waiting in line to begin their long journey up to the top of the two towers, only to meet their unfathomable fate on the way up; the announcement over the TV that every single aircraft in the country was being forced to land at the nearest airport by the President of the United States, to rule out the possibility of another attack; the equally as shocking news that another plane was heading straight for Washington, D.C., perhaps the White House or our nation's Capitol; turned out to be the Pentagon. And then came the final straw that launched the attacks on Iraq and the search for Osama bin Laden.

First one tower crumbled to the ground, causing yet another 'Oh my God' moment, and about a half hour later the second one met exactly the same fate. How could this happen? How could any of this have happened? So many questions: Who? Why? How? So many innocent lives were lost. We may never know all the answers. Just like the JFK assassination plot, conspiracy theories abounded. Firefighters became the new national heroes and rightfully so. The ones who stood bravely in line in order to rescue however many lives they possibly could, even after the first tower fell, gave new meaning to their old credo of *'Who else would walk into a burning building when everyone else is trying to run out?'* And then that final image of all the people within a mile of the towers trying to get out of the city, crossing over the Hudson River by foot on the Brooklyn Bridge. As that horrible nightmare of a day came to dusk, the New York City skyline was black with smoke from the total destruction of their most famous landmark. And nothing would ever be the same.

As incredible as the events of that morning had been, I still had to go to the truck stop at 3:00 in the afternoon.

It was still America, they didn't attack our capital, and life went on. When I got there you could tell everyone was wondering what would happen next. It turned out to be a pretty normal day work-wise but the repercussions would not be felt by the trucking industry for another few months, as the domino effect took hold of the rest of the country. It took a while, but a year later the evenings of working on trucks till midnight every night and staying busy the rest of the afternoon were over. By October 2002 we had four mechanics in the bays from 3:00 till 11:00pm every Monday through Thursday. Some afternoons there would be a total of only six to eight trucks. Something was telling me this job was not going to last much longer. But I still needed the extra money to pay off my credit card debt. So I hung in there with the other mechanics and shared the work or lack thereof. I knew they wouldn't miss me if I left. It would just mean more work for them. It seemed a shame to have to end my brief career as a mechanic in this manner. But none of us were making any money. I had learned a lot in the two short years I worked on big rigs. And now it seemed I would have to find another job. I didn't really feel like going back to golf course maintenance again, but by now you know my situation.

Wait on the Lord: be of good courage, and he shall strengthen thine heart: wait, I say, on the Lord.

Psalm 27:14 (KJV)

Surfing, motocross, and my daughter were what the 1980's were all about.

(Top) My daughter and I reunited over at my brother's home in 1987.
(Bottom) Our trip to Georgia in 1995 at my mom's home in Ellijay.

(Top) My first 5K in Orlando 1992. (Bottom) My dad and I in 2004.

Our honeymoon in Georgia. February, 2005.

Cocoa Beach 5K in 2005.

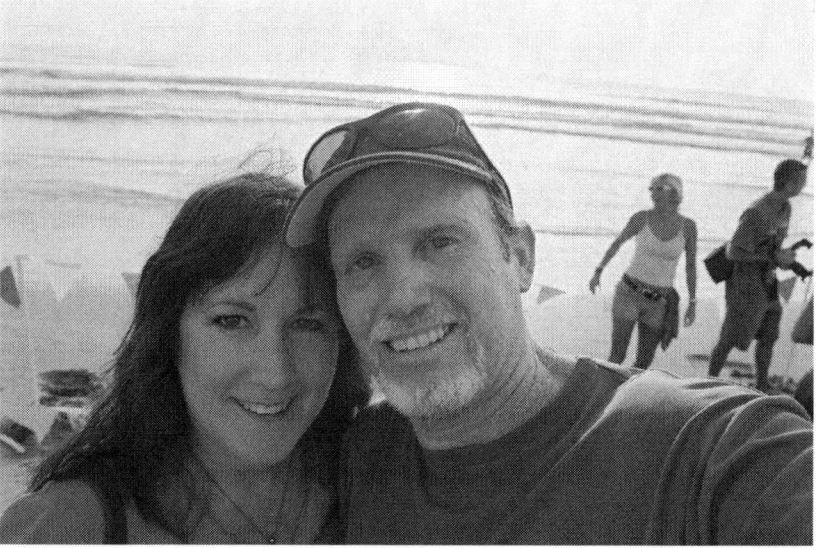

After the beach run on Cocoa Beach with Kelly, September 2005.

My visit to North Carolina in February of 2009 to see my daughter.

Playing hockey in Orlando in 2008.

On my way to the 'high country' of North Carolina in 2009.

The tiny waterfall at the top of the mountain in North Carolina.

This is the exact spot where God spoke to me on the mountaintop.

My eye after I got hit with a hockey stick.

Playing goalie for the Can Ams in 2011, first time.

205

Taking a shot from one of the Lyons players, Can Ams vs. Lyons 2011.

My wife loves to take pictures of nature. This was on Cocoa Beach.

Cocoa Beach surfing on my birthday in 2015.

Running with my sister near our home in Central Florida, 2013.

Me, my sister, and my brother (L to R) in our living room, 2015.

(Top) Praising God while out on a trail run.
(Bottom) Finishing up a half marathon in Pensacola in 2014.

Playing in the orchestra in Orlando, 2015 and 2016.

Mom and my brother Gar came to watch me play in 2016.

Overlooking God's country in North Carolina, 2016.

Another trip up to visit my daughter in Asheville, 2016.

Back in the rookie league in Orlando, 2019.

Playing goalie for the Can Ams for the second time, August 2019.

Facing off against the Lyons in 2019. Best game of my life.

My office by the lake, May 2020.

11 A SPIRITUAL REBUILD BY THE GRACE OF GOD

One morning before work my best friend John came over to shoot the breeze, and I lamented to him how I really wished I could afford to work only one job. He liked to joke about how I used to say I was only working "part-time" since quitting the golf course, from 80-plus hours a week to just 68 hours a week between working at the hospital and the truck stop. He always thought that was pretty funny, but the truth was it really did feel like part-time compared to all the years I worked from sunup to 11:00 at night Monday through Friday and several hours on the weekends too. I guess you could say without hesitation that between the ages of 32 and 42 I had ZERO free time aside from annual vacations, which always felt like absolute blessings from God.

Best friends and neighbors since grade school, we always wished only the best for each other throughout our lives and always helped each other out whenever we could to achieve our goals. Our careers have taken us in different directions, and there have been a few years that we saw very little of each other but our friendship has always been one that picks up wherever we left off no matter how long it has been. So I confessed to him,

"Man I just wish I had more time to do the things I've always wanted to do. I mean I appreciate not having to go to work until 3:00 in the afternoon, it's WAY better than it used to be. But I don't even know what I would do if I actually had a couple of days off each week. I don't know what that would be like."

"Yeah, I've got to admit, I don't know how you've done it all these years. How long have you had two jobs?" asked John.

"Two full-time jobs for about, uh, let's see.....I guess about seven years, since '95 when I left school," I said.

"And how long did your dad have two jobs?" he asked.

"Not sure, he had that job at Goodyear for a couple of years at least, you know, plus working at the Plant. What, are you trying to say I'm a harder worker than my dad was? Forget it man. That man lives to work, not me!"

John laughed. He always got such a kick out of how I saw myself differently from how he saw me.

"Just sayin' man, you're always saying you're not like your dad," John said, trying to talk and laugh at the same time. "And look at you! You've turned out just like him!"

"I'm NOT like him, man. It just seems like that but I've had to work two jobs for all these years just to afford this house. If it weren't for that second job I'd still be living in those old apartments downtown," I said.

When John's laughter finally died down a bit he started asking me questions like how much equity I had in my home, how much money would I need to pay off my credit cards, and other financial stuff. Long story short, he recommended I go talk to his wife, who was a mortgage officer at a local bank.

"I'm telling you Rick, you need to go talk to her, she really knows her stuff. You might just be able to pay off some of those credit cards with the equity in your home."

And that is exactly how it happened. With the help of my best friend and his wife I was able to pay off almost all of my credit card debt, so much so that I figured I could quit one of my jobs if I wanted to. It seemed like nothing short of a miracle to me at the time. The only question would be, "Which job should I keep and which one should I quit?"

By the middle of November 2002 all my financial troubles of the past were taken care of. It seemed like a miracle and maybe it was. God had used my best friend John to help me break free of my financial burdens so that I would never forget what a good friend he had been my whole life. I could likely never repay him, short of one day laying my life down for him as Scripture says in John 15:13.

Greater love has no one than this: to lay down one's life for one's friends. (NIV)

I knew then that I was definitely going to quit one of my jobs. I was burned out both physically and mentally and was ready for a break. The job at the hospital had been providing insurance benefits for both my daughter and me since she was 7 years old in 1990. But now she was 19 and could get her own benefits. I seldom used mine, as I had been blessed by God to be strong and healthy for most of my life. So I was pretty sure I was going to put in two weeks notice at the hospital and keep working at the truck stop in order to obtain an ASE certification in diesel mechanics. I figured that to be a good decision, one I could live and grow with.

The third week of November came, and we suffered through another Monday night with only a handful of trucks to keep the four of us busy. I think I made about $30.00 commission that night for eight hours of working and waiting. The next afternoon when I got to the shop there were only about five or six semis in the parking lot waiting for service. I thought maybe business would pick up a little by nightfall. It didn't. We were all sitting around waiting for some work when a truck pulled in needing a trailer tire changed. I got the nod. I don't know why but by the time I had the trailer jacked up and had grabbed the big air hammer to loosen the lug nuts, I knew this was going to be my last job I would perform as a diesel mechanic. When I got the wheel off the hub, rolled it over to the middle of the bay and dropped it on the floor, I looked up at the head mechanic, who was still sitting on a stool waiting for work, and I said,

"This is my last job, O.J."

That was his name. When anyone ever chided him about it (and they usually did) he always asked if they wanted his autograph. He had been there since long before I started working there, the rock that kept that shop, especially our shift, from getting buried in our work by the amount of trucks we used to service prior to September 11th, 2001. And there he sat waiting for a single truck to come in so that he could make some money. It was time for me to leave. So I finished changing the tire, said my goodbyes to the mechanics, and loaded up all my tools on the back of my old Chevy

pickup. As I headed home down Route #60, I knew I had
made the right decision. I needed a break from working
seven days a week and now I would get one. The hospital
job was only three 12-hour days, from Friday through
Sunday night. The rest of the week would be mine! I
could hardly believe this was really happening. It felt like
a dream. I felt so free, thanks to the grace of God and
with the help of my best friend John. He would continue
to poke fun at me because I said I was retired even
though I still worked 36 hours/week. It didn't phase my
retirement claim though. Working three full days a week
was a far cry from seven days a week.

So the first thing I did when I pulled into my
driveway as a free man, right after wheeling my large
tool chest into the living room with the help of my next
door neighbor, was to call up my best friend and tell him
the good news. Needless to say he was happy for me. He
had been clearing his new lot to build a home for his new
bride and himself when I called. He told me to come on
over, so we sat on the huge John Deere front-end loader
the rest of the evening, drank a couple beers to celebrate,
and just chewed the fat how old buddies do; didn't talk

about anything in particular, just had a few laughs and a good time. I left his new lot that evening with a slight buzz and a big smile on my face. For the first time since I was a young man there was something to look forward to besides more work.

But what to do with all of my newfound freedom? It had been totally unplanned, and I had been a planner for as far back as I remember. The plan had been to work at the truck stop for another five years and then scale back to work at only the hospital until retirement. Heck, I had even contemplated at one time working both jobs for another twenty years and then retiring with one heck of a retirement fund. What had changed my mind? God's grace and the promise of freedom. Jesus said,

"Come to me, all you who are weary and burdened, and I will give you rest."

Matthew 11:28 (NIV)

When I awoke the morning of that first day of my new life, it still hadn't fully registered how truly free I was. I found myself still planning out the days, until the end of that first day. Then it finally hit me. I was free as a bird, at least until the weekends. Mondays through

Thursdays I could do anything. It was a little difficult to grasp. But it wasn't like I could just go anywhere and do anything as if I had retired with an unlimited cash flow. Money was going to be scarce. There would be just enough for a house payment and the usual essential bills each month. I wasn't about to go back into debt, ever again. I would have about $100.00/month to play with and that was it. What could I do? One thing I had always wanted to try if I ever got to totally retire was to learn to catch fish. This would be the perfect opportunity. So I set out to start a new hobby, fishing, and I wanted to do it right. The plan was to buy a cane pole and use my bicycle to ride down to the river with a bait bucket and cooler attached to a rack on the back of the bike. If I caught any fish I would put them on ice in the cooler, ride back home and cook them up for supper. And do you know what? The plan worked! I found a favorite fishing hole where every time I went I would catch red snapper, saltwater trout, or Spanish mackerel. I became quite the fisherman, and my kitchen smelled so much like fish that I had to lay off the cooking for a week to give it a break. Everything felt so right, as if God was giving me that special time to enjoy my life like I hadn't been able to since I first started surfing about 25 years earlier. I caught fish all the way from January through the end of April while the weather was perfect for fishing or doing anything else outdoors. Some mornings I would wake up really early, around 4:00am, and take the old Chevy truck to the Sebastian Inlet to catch some sand fleas (mole crabs) that would roll in with the tide down by the south jetty. I can't even express the feeling of arriving at the beach before sunrise, chasing down sand fleas and scooping them up in a basket as they showed up in bushels whenever the water got sucked back out into the shorebreak. It's about as close to Heaven as you will ever find with your baggies on, short of surfing anyway. So peaceful, so innocent; so free.

Inevitably the perfect weather of winter and springtime in Florida diminished and the harsh reality of summer took their place. The miracle of that special time in my life is but a distant memory now, yet I believe I am a different person having experienced it because I know the true meaning of the word *serendipity*. According to Wikipedia, serendipity is *the occurrence of an unplanned fortunate discovery,* and it describes to a tee what happened to me right after I retired from the truck stop. I never dreamed the simple act of fishing could provide such peace, inner joy, and overall contentment. If the weather could stay perfect year-round in Florida I may never have stopped fishing the Indian River. That's just how addicting it was. But the Florida summers are way too hot and sunny for this Canadian transplant with Irish skin. So I had to come up with an alternate plan for May through November. I knew one thing: I was still burned out from working two jobs since my daughter was born. There was no way I was going to look for another job to use up all my recently acquired spare time. But I wasn't the type to ever just sit home and watch TV or surf the internet either.

Before I had even cast out my last shrimp of the season into the salty water of my favorite fishing hole in Vero Beach in the spring of 2003, I knew what I wanted to do with those four days off during the week: go back to college and complete my associate's degree. It had seemed like such a waste to have come so far and then just quit for good. Even though I had zero interest in getting back into radiography, I wanted to get back to school and finish a degree program. Honestly, it didn't even matter which program. The hospital would pay for any and all classes as long as they led to a degree, so I definitely wanted to take advantage of that. Heck, what could it hurt? The catch was that I was still living in a small town, they had a limited amount of degrees available for transfer into a university, and I had been setting my sights on an eventual bachelor's degree. I had a new outlook on life and the sky was the limit.

I decided on an Associate of Arts degree since they seemed to be more flexible and I have never been much of a scientist anyway. The local college was so close to my little house that I rode a bicycle to classes four days a week, graduating with honors from community college in 2004; what a year! Met my future wife in January and told her about my future plans of finishing college with a bachelor's degree in something, didn't know what yet. She told me she would back me in anything I set out to accomplish. Times were tough at first. I had been living basically by myself for almost twenty years. That's a long time. It wouldn't take a genius to realize I could have gone on living the rest of my life as a bachelor, unhitched and untethered, free as the wind. But as I had told my best friend John one day on the way to the river on one of our fishing trips, I had everything my heart had ever desired out of life: a home, time to enjoy life, the love of my daughter, and a new grandchild. The only thing I lacked was someone to share it with. I needed a woman. Paul wrote this to the Church in Corinth concerning a single man contemplating marriage:

Now to the unmarried and the widows I say: It is good for them to stay unmarried, as I do. But if they cannot control themselves, they should marry, for it is better to marry than to burn with passion.

1 Corinthians 7:8-9

He goes on to write that a married couple will experience many troubles in this life. As a single man, ever since I was young I always burned with passion. Sometimes I wish I never had that much passion. But then passionate people always seem to be more alive and energetic. So maybe it's a blessing, I don't know. But that first year was really difficult for us. Throw in the dual hurricanes of 2004, Frances and Jeanne, and we have both wondered out loud since then how we are even still together. We just celebrated 15 years of marriage this year, and thank God our toughest year has still been that first one.

Concerning those two hurricanes if I may, allow me to elaborate just a bit. Neither one was a Katrina or Andrew, or I guess the new standard is the storm that all but obliterated Puerto Rico in 2017, Hurricane Maria; but they did their fair share of destruction to the east coast of Florida, and it was said that not one city in the state was spared the wrath from at least one named storm that year. As Floridians we learned to respect the aftermath almost as much as the storm itself. Yet God was more than merciful and gracious to us throughout the storm and its aftermath. It was downright miraculous how He left my tiny house almost untouched throughout the storm's fury while other homes up and down the east coast were not so fortunate. He truly answered my pre-hurricane prayer in a way most favorable to our survival in the aftermath. As the first hurricane, Frances, bore down on us, with the windows all boarded up and the anxiety starting to build, my fiancé asked if I would say a prayer for us before the storm actually hit. I gathered my thoughts, we kneeled by the foot of the bed, bowed our heads, and I prayed something like this:

"Dear Father, we ask that you please watch over our house during the storm, and our families and friends as well. We ask that you bring us through this hurricane and keep us safe. We know that this is your storm and not the devil's. If it is your will to see us through, please keep us safe. But if it is your will to take us in this storm, please forgive us for all our sins Father. We ask this all in Jesus' name, Amen."

God must have found favor in my prayer because none of our family or friends were harmed during the storm, though some of their homes were damaged rather severely, nothing however that was beyond repair. As for my little house that everyone suggested I abandon before the storm got within 100 miles? It lost about five shingles from the hip-style roof. My new aluminum shed was demolished from fallen Australian pines, yet nothing inside of it was damaged in the least. The yard was a disaster, no getting around that. And after the second storm blew through three weeks later, all the yards were flooded for about a month. We were without power for a total of a month, but by the time the second storm (Jeanne) had passed, the weather was a lot cooler than it had been after Frances. Trying to sleep with no air conditioning or fan in the middle of September anywhere in Florida is miserable. My only respite was when I got to go to the hospital on the weekends and enjoy the air conditioning and hot food. Other than that it was a long month and a half. Thank God for friends and family. And thanks be to God for His grace, which is always sufficient.

The following year was much better. There was another hurricane but it blew through in about an hour, not long enough to do any substantial damage. A really bad hurricanc usually hangs around for about ten hours or so, some even longer. A lot of people describe them as if the devil pays their town a visit, but we must keep in mind that God creates hurricanes and tornadoes just as He creates rainbows, sunny days, and perfect days for fishing. Only when we realize that can we feel totally protected, even in the midst of a storm.

When I think of the year 2005 I will always think of my marriage to the first woman who ever really loved me and continues to do so even today. We spent our honeymoon in Ellijay, Georgia where my mother was living with my step dad at the time. It was a wonderful wedding and trip. The weather was perfect, a blend of sunshine, clouds, fog, rain, and even snow, something my lovely bride had never before experienced and I had not seen since 1966, short of that brief moment in time it snowed in Florida in 1977. (That had been pretty bizarre too.) We threw snowballs at each other while the dog licked the falling snowflakes out of the fresh mountain air. Of course it was great to see my mom again. She really appreciated that we wanted to spend time with her and her husband on that special occasion. As we left Ellijay and that incredible week behind us in the rear view mirror and headed back to Florida, it was time to start our new lives together as a couple. We had been living together for several months so it was kind of like business as usual once we got back home, except of course now we were 'official.' Nothing really earth-shattering occurred while we were newlyweds. We enjoyed going down to the river in the evenings after work and sitting on a bench while watching the sun go down over the small town of Vero Beach. Forever the romantic one between the two of us, my wife could always find somewhere to go where we could take along a picnic lunch, breakfast, or even dinner. I had started running in my spare time as well, a pastime I had enjoyed competing in some twelve years earlier, having run seven races during the fall of 1992/winter of '93, including my first race through downtown Orlando, the old Dick Batchelor Run for the Children 5K. Five kilometers was definitely my favorite distance, and I seldom finished out of the top ten overall at any given local race, with an average time of around 18:30. My best race of all time, speed-wise, was a run by the Sebastian River on a cold winter morning in the middle of February, 1993. It would be the last competitive race I would run until July 4th weekend in 2005. The wind was blowing pretty hard out of the north, bringing the 'feels like' temperature down into the 30's. Most runners were wearing face protection in the form of either handkerchiefs or Vaseline-type salves to prevent windburn. My main competitor, a naturally-gifted runner from New York named Joe, even offered me some Vaseline for my face, but I thanked him and turned it down. I've always hated to smear any kind of greasy stuff on my face, or any other part of my body for that matter. The race started with a bang, as a lot of them do, with a little over 100 runners braving the cold. We took off into the brisk wind, sort of a mixed blessing whether one is riding a bicycle or running a race. Since it was basically an out-and-back course with very little deviation from a straight road that paralleled the river, I relished the thought that the wind would be totally at our backs once we turned around at the halfway point and headed to the finish line. Not to mention I was going to try out a new strategy I had been practicing during the previous week. Instead of trying to keep up with Joe or any other fast runner during the race, and then inevitably not having enough steam left to pass them if necessary down the stretch, I would try something new. I don't even remember reading about it anywhere; it came to me one day on my favorite trail in Riverside Park on the Indian River. I loved that trail. Chuck and I used to train on it twice a week during the 'year that was' 1980

Florida motocross series. Anyway, I decided to keep a fast but easy pace, one I could run without too much exertion, keeping close tabs on my stopwatch on the way back. When the watch read 17:00 minutes I would take off on a sprint to the finish line. It was a bit of a gamble but it seemed to work pretty well in practice. Well it worked out even better during the race. I had longer legs than Joe. He was more of a fast and steady runner who relied on a super quick pace to pass other runners throughout a race. I had always counted on my 'kick', which usually began within the last 75 to 100 yards. This time however, it would begin when the clock struck 17:00 minutes. Joe passed me up in the last two minutes of the race, something I had been expecting; that was usually his strategy. He would use me as the rabbit to adjust his speed and then just turn it up a bit when the time came. He knew he had to pass me early enough that he wouldn't have to race me down the stretch. He just couldn't beat me in a finish line dash. Joe gave me sort of a wave as he ran by and I just nodded and waved back. I'm pretty sure he was a bit shocked when I didn't put up much of a fight; but I checked my watch and it said we were only 16:45 into the race. It wasn't time yet. Five seconds later another competitor, Mike, passed by and waved. I nodded but acted as if I didn't care. Ten more seconds ticked by and it was 17:00; GO TIME. Time to put the hammer down. Racers have 100 different ways of saying it but they all mean the same thing: time to haul ass. I started running as fast as I could and told myself I wasn't slowing down until I passed the finish line. First I blew by Mike, then I passed Joe like he was on a Sunday evening jog. Next thing I know the finish line banner is only about a 50 yard dash away. One of the fastest runners at any race, a guy my age named Jeff, who usually finished in the 17minute-plus range, was actually within my reach. I immediately thought, *if I had only started my kick about 30 seconds sooner,* but there was no time for regrets now. In less than ten seconds the race would be over. I finished in 18:00 minutes flat, my best time ever in the 5K. Both Mike and Joe congratulated me after we had all passed the finish line and were catching our breaths. They seemed amazed that I had improved my personal best by 30 seconds in less than a month. I was kind of amazed as well. I had learned a lot about racing during that short season of seven 5K's. But the season was over, and by the fall I was back to working two jobs again in preparation for college. And like I said, I never raced again competitively until 2005, which brings us to the 5K in Palm Bay, Florida on July 4th weekend. I had been training since the spring of 2004 and wanted to make the Dick Batchelor 5K in October my comeback race; it's always been just about my favorite 5K since 1992. I had even pre-registered and received the commemorative running tank top, since the running store that put on the race was celebrating the 25th anniversary of their locally famous shop that year. But, being in October, it was too soon after the hurricanes and by the time the race went down I hadn't trained in a couple of months. I guess I should have raced anyway but that's never been how I rolled. I have always been adamant about being prepared for every athletic, academic, musical, or work related event I have ever participated in, and have followed my ex-boss/football coach's credo: *Prior planning prevents poor performance.*

So by the time the Palm Bay 5K was on my calendar, I was way more than ready; I was downright jumpy, even though the temperature was about 90 degrees at 8:00 in the morning when the starting gun went off. I decided to run a smart race, nothing fancy; fast enough to reflect my diligent training habits but without the old kick down the final stretch that might risk a muscle tear or tendon pull. After all, the plan was to run as many races as I could find in the area that season, which would officially begin in September/October. Anyway, after a rather conservative race I ended up getting 2nd place in my age group. Naturally I was stoked. What a great way to get back into running! My time was about 21:15 if I remember correctly, a far cry from my heyday back in '92, almost three minutes slower. But it was the middle of summer, my first race since 2001 (a Dick Batchelor 5K once again), and I wasn't pushing it. Not to mention that in the world of amateur athletics, especially running, thirteen years is a long time off. Actually it is a long time, period. I had to face the fact that there was an almost 100% likelihood I would never see 5K times in the teens ever again. Kind of made me appreciate just how fast we had been as 34 year-olds. Anyway, I managed to race about a half dozen more times that season, culminating with a 20:15 effort at the 2nd annual Daytona 5K, a race that used the actual iconic speedway as its venue. That was good enough for a 6th place age group finish. I was okay with that, especially since my old buddy John had journeyed with me to that race and got to see me race two other guys down to the wire and pass them both within 10 yards of the finish line. I still have that photo he shot as we took the checkered flag. Other fun races included one on Cocoa Beach, and I mean right **on** Cocoa Beach, one down by the river by the old trail in Riverside Park, and one we ran through my own neighborhood that finished right smack in the middle of old downtown Vero Beach. Good times, but by the end of that season I was already showing signs of slowing down. Following the thrilling Daytona race in January, my times by the end of April hovered closer to the 20:30 mark; still not bad but it was a bit disappointing to watch them get slower instead of faster. I finished the season injury free, and in the world of sports that is a good thing. Runners have a plethora of nagging potentially chronic injuries, and at the close of

2006 I showed no signs of any of them. It turned out to be a good year all around.

My wife and I enjoyed 2006 as well. I was in my junior year at university and we were excited that there would hopefully be only one more year till graduation and a chance for a better paying career. Of course there were no guarantees. My major was in Psychology and I wasn't sure what one could do with a Bachelor's in Psychology. Heck, I'm still not sure. It's one of those academic degrees that require the student to keep pressing onward until he or she completes at least a master's degree before it can be utilized to its potential. But our arguments were becoming fewer and less severe, and we were settling into our lives together. Her biggest pet peeve had long been her claim that I was still clinging to my independence. I had been under the impression that one could remain independent while staying married, as long as each spouse respected the other. That philosophy had always caused a riff between us, as my wife had never been much of an independent person, even when she was single. I want to tell you, this is a major difference in philosophies and lifestyles, and has been one of the most polarizing aspects of our relationship since day one. Had it not been for my ever growing relationship with God, Jesus, and the Holy Spirit, I don't know how I could have ever changed my philosophy and gradually matured enough through time to realize that perhaps my wife had been right all along about my independence interfering with our marriage vows. It's true that couples who stay together often have to change together. Some couples may have met under common circumstances, others under common interests, and some just seem to hit it off like old friends from the very start. No matter now they meet, people change over the years. The Bible says married couples are to love each other *for better or for worse.* Scripture also says, in both the Old and New Testaments, that after a man leaves his parents to marry, he and his wife become one.

'For this reason a man will leave his mother and father and be united to his wife, and the two will become one flesh.' So they are no longer two, but one flesh. Therefore what God has joined together, let no one separate. - Mark 10:7-9 (NIV)

There was also something very special about 2006 that no one could have ever foreseen, except for God. Toward the end of the year, with a college GPA of 3.93 in Psychology, and only lacking seven classes toward the degree, my wife and I decided to start looking forward to our future. Having felt that a Bachelor's in Psychology could only lead to a master's program, I began searching for just that, and found one at a university in Jacksonville (FL). It was a paid internship in Rehabilitation Counseling, tuition-free to anyone accepted into the program. When I told my wife about it she agreed it would be a perfect fit if I were accepted. Next, a funny thing happened. I had remembered from a wedding we attended in Jacksonville that there was an ice rink somewhere on the outskirts of the city. I became excited about the possibility of ice skating and maybe even playing hockey again, something I hadn't even considered after moving down to Florida in 1966, forty years earlier. The idea seemed incredible, ludicrous, and yet highly possible, as long as I got accepted into university in Jacksonville. But there was more to the story. I decided to check online for other rinks in Florida, just in case the college plan fell through. And lo and behold, I found one in Rockledge, about an hour's drive north on I-95 from my house in Vero. That was it; my reincarnation as a late-blooming hockey player/goalie began right then and there. We drove up to Rockledge to check out the rink and drove back home with as much hockey equipment as I could afford to buy during that first visit. Before I even got out on the ice again after 40 years I had all the equipment necessary to play in the NHL. All I lacked were the skills. First thing I did was join a novice league that met every Tuesday evening to scrimmage. What a blast! It was like being a kid again. I never knew much about positioning in hockey when I was a kid, and 40 years later I still didn't know where I was supposed to be or what I was supposed to be doing. But I seemed to have an instinct for chasing the puck so they let me play center most of the time. My favorite thing to do was take faceoffs; it made me feel important, like a playmaker or captain or something. And of course I would run into Canadians all the time. There was an ongoing saying in all the locker rooms that if you ever wanted to know where Canadians hang out in Florida, just go to a hockey rink. Didn't seem too far off. I loved everything about going to the rink. The scent as you enter into the ice arena from the lounge out front is an odor that is embedded inside the olfactory lobes of every kid who was ever a Pee Wee, a Tyke, or a junior hockey player. It is totally indescribable unless you grew up skating or playing at an indoor rink. As soon as I step into the double doors at our local rink here in Central Florida, it always reminds me of every time I ever laced up the skates and hit the ice since the age of five. For however long I am at the rink, whether watching a game, playing, or just skating, I am a kid again. That's the only way I can describe it. And you know what Jesus said about the innocence of a child:

And He said: "Truly I tell you, unless you change and become like little children, you will never enter the kingdom of heaven."

Matthew 18:3 (NIV)

If God ever takes me while I am playing hockey, I will surely go to Heaven.

So that was the surprise ending to an already great year for us. As it came to a close I couldn't wait to see what the year 2007 would bring. There were so many new opportunities on the horizon. The first big thing the new year brought would turn out to be huge. I received a letter in the mail one day with a college logo on the top left corner of the envelope, the same college I had applied to a couple of months earlier. My wife watched intently as I slowly opened it up. By that time I had received about the same number of rejection letters as letters of acceptance, so I was well aware that it could go either way. But there was no question once the letter was opened what kind it was. The first word after 'Dear Richard' was '**Congratulations.**' My wife and I were both excited. This year would be a time for change, a time to start a new chapter in our lives. My studies would continue, but no longer for a random subject that might lead nowhere. Now there would be a definite direction, an actual career to shoot for while attending a new school in a brand new city. It was definitely an exciting time to be in our shoes. My wife just wanted to make sure to tie up one loose end before we left our small town behind and headed to Jacksonville. We had both been taking advantage of the great insurance benefits that came with the territory as a healthcare worker. We had good dental, medical, and a decent retirement plan with employer contributions. Yet my wife had not taken advantage of the free cancer screenings and was overdue for a mammogram. I'm guessing they were still pretty painful in those days and a lot of women would keep putting them off. So she set up an appointment with her doctor for a mammogram and we waited for the results. I wasn't too worried because I couldn't imagine anything bad could happen to us at that point; I mean everything had been going so smoothly since our relationship had improved, you know? You can just tell sometimes when God is behind you in all your goals. But my wife was a little worried. She had felt a lump on her breast that would not go away, and it naturally bothered her quite a bit. I won't go into the details because she explains everything very clearly in her spiritual book *"Imminent Rapture"* (Hughes, Kelly, 2019). But it affected our plans so I will tell you the result of her cancer screening. Her doctor brought us into a small room and sat us down together. Then he stood in front of us and gave us the news: the lump on her breast was malignant and she would require surgery. We were both stunned. My wife cried and told me she was so sorry. All of our plans would have to be put on hold, but that was fine with me as long as my wife would be okay. All the plans I had made were for both of us. After all, when I had prayed for a woman four years earlier, I had everything I had ever wanted out of life: a decent job, close friends and family and the freedom to pursue my hobbies. All I lacked was a woman, and that is exactly why I went to God with my request. And that is why even to this day, whenever I think life would be simpler as a bachelor, I remember that I was once what I would consider one of the luckiest bachelors alive, and I prayed to God for a woman. Women may not always make life easier but they do make it a lot less lonely, and that was something I knew plenty about. So yeah, we were in this together, no matter what.

Her surgery was in February and according to the doctor was a complete success, rendering my wife cancer free. We both breathed a lot easier knowing that her life had been spared, but the next few months would be tough. Chemo treatments, secondary surgeries, not to mention her hair falling out, were all precursors to what was in store for us in the months ahead. One day at a doctor's office, I stood by helplessly as she lay on an examining table almost bleeding to death after a surgeon's tiny misjudgment with a scalpel. He had left the room following his incision, not knowing he had nicked an artery, and upon his return noticed the pool of blood on the floor beneath the table she lay upon. She was immediately rushed to the emergency room. When I tell you we had a rough start to 2007 I am not kidding around. And I had almost zero time to take care of my wife, although she appreciated every little thing I did for her, including sitting down beside her during chemo treatments. It was actually pretty easy, as the room where the chemo was administered was directly adjacent to my department in the hospital. Whenever she was receiving a treatment I would sneak away for a few minutes to keep her company. She really liked that and it was the very least I could do. But back to having very little spare time; I had decided to try to finish up my degree in the spring semester, mostly in order to free up my schedule so that I could take care of my wife in any way that she might need me. Seven classes remained toward the degree, the most I had ever tried to tackle in one semester. It required focus, dedication, and organization, and it wasn't easy by any means. But through sheer determination and with the help of a couple of awesome college professors who knew what we were going through, I graduated university in May of 2007 with a Bachelor of Arts in Psychology. It was bittersweet for sure. Whenever I would think about what might have been had I been able to go to Rehabilitation Counseling school in Jacksonville, I often prayed to God and asked Him to show me what I was supposed to be shooting for since that dream had been shattered. I waited for His answer and when it did not come I decided to look for a part-time job to supplement my income, which had recently become the sole source of income in our household since my wife had to quit her job, at least temporarily. I found one at the small hospital in the town north of us. I would be working in their sterile processing department per diem Mondays through Thursdays and at our hospital on the weekends, Fridays through Sundays. I hadn't thought I would ever have to work two jobs again after quitting the truck stop, but throughout life you've always got to roll with the punches and do what you got to do.

And if all that wasn't enough to make me want to just skip right over 2007 and start in 2008, we got a call one evening in early July that Dad had fallen down in the kitchen and was in the emergency room with a possible fractured hip. A few days later he was undergoing total hip surgery at our hospital. When we all went to see him after surgery he seemed to be in good spirits, joking around with all the pretty nurses, putting aside any pain he might have been experiencing. That was my dad. His wit was still there but his wits did not all seem to be. He may have suffered a reaction to the anesthesia after such a long drawn out surgery. I was told that some elderly patients do not recover fully after being anesthetized during surgery. I wasn't aware of that previously. Some of the things he was saying didn't make much sense. A few days later he was moved to hospice. I was so naive back then I didn't even know what hospice was. When I found out Dad wouldn't be coming out of there alive, I had to excuse myself from his bedside in front of my brother. I hurried into the tiny bathroom in my dad's room and cried like a baby. When the crying finally ceased I walked back out and apologized.

"Sorry Gar."

My brother was like, '*Pshhht.*'

"Don't worry about it Rick. I've been doing the same thing."

And what was there to be ashamed of? This was the man whom I had idolized as a child, looked up to as a teenager, befriended in my twenties, and tried to impress my whole life. He was everything I thought a man should be: strong but not boastful, kind yet not a pushover, intelligent but not a bookworm, hard working and mechanically inclined. The only trait I wished he would have had was that of a Christian. It hadn't concerned me much when I was younger because my siblings and I hadn't been raised in the church since we left Toronto, so we hardly ever heard about God or Jesus while growing up. But later on, after growing closer to God and the Holy Spirit, I was kind of hoping that deep down inside my dad's heart, the heart of a really good man, there would be a devout Christian. Yet his stubbornness was stronger than his desire to let Christ into his heart. So as we all stood there watching him deteriorate with each passing day, we all prayed that God would take his soul. And you know what? On his last day here on Earth, an Anglican priest came to pray for Dad. Someone had found out, and I don't know who, that my dad had come from a family of devout Anglicans. How he lost his faith down the road is anyone's guess, but I suppose they had their own religion-specific prayer and hymn books they would use on a routine basis. Anyway, on that day Dad had been resting peacefully, and his doctor said that this could be the day. And if your parents or any other loved ones are ever in hospice, you will know what *the day* means. So there were four or five of us standing by his bedside as the priest began to pray. I did not recognize the prayer, but I don't claim to know the entire Bible by heart. What happened next is difficult to explain to anyone who wasn't there. When the priest read the first few words of what we assumed to be a key verse in the Anglican canon, my dad raised his head up off his pillow with every little bit of strength left in his dying body and uttered a sort of groaning noise from his lips. And then he lay back down. To this day everyone there swears my dad finally accepted Christ at that very moment. Minutes later, I decided to head back home, having been in the room for a couple of hours paying my respects to the man I could never muster up the courage to say goodbye to. An hour later my brother called to say that Dad was gone. And once again I cried like a baby. My wife and I drove over to our old house where Dad had lived for just over 40 years, his home in Vero Beach, Florida. The same home we grew up in. It's hard to explain the feeling of losing a parent. People say the toughest thing anyone could ever have to do is bury their own child, and I believe that. At least when a parent precedes their children in death, there is comfort in knowing they didn't have to bury their own children. But for the children it is still tough. It's a void that never seems to be filled. Dad passed away at the age of 88.

The rest of the year was spent going through the grieving process. I ran another 5K in September but it was more or less just to divert my attention to something else besides my dad's passing. Next I tried to get back into Jacksonville's counseling program at the college but as luck would have it, they had discontinued the internship after the spring of 2007. There was nothing left to do but apply for a bunch of different jobs online. I was so ready to find a job somewhere else and leave my current life behind. I really just needed to get away for awhile. If I could have afforded to, I would have spent a month or two somewhere in the mountains of Georgia, or Tennessee, or North Carolina, or even Canada. But of course I still had bills to pay. At least my wife Kelly was well enough that she had found another job. That was definitely a plus to an otherwise depressing year. As 2008 rolled around I was just hoping for a change for the better.

It came in January in the form of a phone call from a large hospital in Orlando. Their HR department had received my job application, one of many I had sent out during the previous couple of months, and wanted to know if I would be interested in a position in their sterile processing department as an educator. Apparently their department manager had been impressed by the samples I had included of the newsletter I produced and wrote each month for my local hospital. I called it *"Sterile Prep Times"* and had been distributing it to about seven different department leaders for each month of publication. I always found something interesting to write about sterile processing in each issue. If you'd like to find out more about sterile processing or the seven issues of *"Sterile Prep Times"* I published, they are all included in their entirety in my book **"Sterile Processing, Invisible Culture"** (2019), available on Amazon.com. In the book I also go into further detail about my exploits as a sterile processing educator. So yeah, spoiler alert, but I ended up accepting the position and we moved up to Orlando in 2008 to start a new life.

It was tough leaving our family and friends in Vero after living my whole life there since the age of eight, but I was ready. It's funny how whenever you load up all your belongings on a big truck and move to another town, you feel just like the Beverly Hillbillies leaving their small town in the Tennessee hills. But that's just how the city of Orlando felt compared to Vero Beach. I really enjoyed the difference, at least at first, when it was all new. My new boss was great, she couldn't have made me feel any more welcome. And I loved teaching young people the job I had been doing for almost twenty years.

The hospital was so big they gave me a classroom to teach in on Mondays. The rest of the week I taught from inside the sterile processing department. I thought from the beginning that I had finally found my niche in life, my purpose, and that God had placed me in that job as both an answered prayer and a new mission. The first few months were pure satisfaction on the job. I was making good money, the same as I had been making while working two jobs in Vero. There was no reason to believe I would ever leave that job for any other, all the way to retirement, but that was still at least 17 years down the road. But I should have remembered the old adage: If something seems too good to be true, it probably isn't. Toward the end of the year (2008) my boss began treating me differently and expecting more out of me, more than I thought I could give. We got into arguments, bad ones, almost daily, and I would come home from work each day ranting and raving about my job assignments and the boss. It got so bad my wife just told me one day, hey do what you've got to do. There were reasons my supervisor was acting differently toward me and expecting more out of me, and I don't lay 100%

of the blame on her. I can't reveal them in this book because it is a matter of respecting someone's privacy and the company's too. But it didn't matter the reason. I enjoyed being the educator and was proud to have achieved that status after working so many years as a tech in such a small town. It was as if getting a degree had really paid off. But I just couldn't do the job if my supervisor was going to keep piling everything on my shoulders relentlessly day after day with no one restraining her from doing so. It wasn't fair to me or my wife, and I wanted to live to see retirement some day. So I put in my two weeks notice, she told me to pack my bags, and I was gone and never looked back. Another chapter in my life, my *new* life, was over, this time without a new one to follow. I had nothing up my sleeves, no backup, no plan B, nothing. I was out of work for the first time in my adult life. Funny thing is I was happy. The job had been so mentally draining on me that it was a relief to finally be over it and not have to worry or stress about it anymore. That was an indication to me that I had made the right decision. The only question was what to do next.

It was January 2009, the beginning of a new year, the time I usually liked to plan new ideas, even under normal circumstances. This year was no different except the biggest plan had to be finding another job, during a recession no less. I applied at a few places but had no idea where I was supposed to go or what I was supposed to do. By mid-February I was volunteering for the Red Cross and also at a museum in Orlando. So at least I was learning some new skills. Then one afternoon my ex-wife called our apartment out of the blue and said my daughter had been going through a tough time and was asking for me. Since I had all the time in the world at that point, my wife urged me to drive up and visit her. Kelly was working at a department store in Orlando and I would have to make the journey on my own. My head sure could have used clearing out anyway, so I was packed and on my way to the hills of North Carolina within an hour.

It was nice to get away for awhile. I had no idea how long I would be gone but the feeling of hitting the open road has long been known to rejuvenate the soul and free up the spirit. I thought maybe God might take that opportunity to communicate some sort of message or give me some kind of sign because my mind was an open slate at that point just waiting for the Holy Spirit to enter into it. But the ride up to North Carolina turned out to be pretty uneventful, just a smooth relaxing journey into the Great Smoky Mountains. I spent a few days up there enjoying the cool weather and the heavenly scenery and got the chance to spend some time with my 26 year-old daughter who was still searching for her own soul. It's true what they say that being a parent never ends, even after your kids grow up. I tried to always act respectable whenever in my daughter's presence and I think I've done a pretty good job of it. Nobody makes the perfect parent; we all have our shortcomings, but my daughter still knows to this day she can always count on me for love and support whenever she needs it. What she really needed at that particular time was just to talk and spend some time with her dad. Daughters may act all grown up when they are around their mothers, but they are always daddy's little girl when he is around. We enjoyed our time together and as always, it was difficult to leave her behind, but she had made the choice a year earlier to leave Florida behind and move closer to her mother. It's never been easy for either of us, and sometimes I realize it has led to some of her psychological problems. I know it took years for me to come to terms with the fact that us being separated as a family at her very young age would likely affect my daughter's entire life. And I would not have blamed anyone for calling me irresponsible, uncaring, or an unfit dad. God knows that in my twenties that description fit me pretty well, except for the uncaring part. I never stopped caring about my daughter. I worked as hard as I could for as many hours a week as I could stand until the day she no longer lived with her mother or me, just to provide for both her and myself. And since then Jesus has lifted the burden of guilt from my shoulders and laid it upon His own. He set me free. And I will go on supporting her for as long as she needs me, even if only to make sure she knows that there is a God up in Heaven that loves her, and a friend named Jesus whom she can call on at any time to help her get through anything.

But he was pierced for our transgressions,
  he was crushed for our iniquities;

the punishment that brought us peace was on him,
and by his wounds we are healed.   Isaiah 53:5

It was difficult but we eventually did say our goodbyes. I dropped her off at her mom's, where she had been staying for the past couple months since she broke up with her boyfriend. It felt like old times, when I used to drop her off after a weekend together back in Vero Beach. We had spent many a Saturday or Sunday at the beach, and I had even taken her up to Cocoa Beach a few times to watch surf contests together and show her around my favorite beach town. I don't imagine we could have spent much more time together on weekends even if we had been together as a family. It wasn't a 'normal' family life but I think we made the best of it.

When I dropped my daughter off at her mom and step dad's house on the other side of the mountain, my ex-wife told me I'd better be heading out if I planned on making it over 'the high country', as they called it, where my motel had been. There was a storm rolling in from the north and it was supposed to be bringing frigid temperatures, ice, and even some possible snow. As a Florida boy not used to that kind of weather, I wasn't going to hang around and wait to see what it was like to drive on the mountains in the ice and snow. So I left for the high country by early afternoon to allow plenty of time to get back to the motel before nightfall. When I got to the top of the mountain it was so breathtakingly beautiful up there, I just had to park the Jeep on the overlook parking area and get out. There were huge icicles, larger than I ever remember seeing as a kid in Toronto, dripping down the rocky cliffs next to the highway. It must have snowed sometime earlier up there because there was still a dusting on the grass on the other side of the highway close to the overlook. I walked over to the snow, stood on a small patch of ice, and snapped a picture of my feet in the ice and snow. I mean, what else do you do, right? Selfies weren't a big thing in 2009, so I took a picture of my feet in the snow and ice. Then I heard the distinct sound of water trickling downhill and followed the enchanting sound to a small waterfall just on the other side of the guardrail by the overlook. I had to investigate. There wasn't much time left before the sun would disappear on the other side of the mountaintop, but I had to at least snap a few pictures of this magical little brook that was cascading crystal clear water down the side of the mountaintop. As I knelt down by the brook for a better perspective, something happened next that I shall never forget. I heard a loud deep rumbling sound not unlike the steady rolling thunder that precedes a hurricane in Florida. So I dismissed it as just that for a few seconds. But the steady rumbling did not go away after a few seconds. In fact it kept rolling for another couple of minutes, long enough for me to stand up from a kneeling position and walk carefully back up to the clearing where I had parked the Jeep. The rumbling sound grew louder as I looked out over the valley and across the mountaintops. I knew then and there that what I was hearing was not ordinary thunder, or a distant jet, or even a squadron of fighter jets on an exercise. No, this steady rumbling sound coming from just over the next mountaintop was none other than God, the great I Am. I had journeyed to this mountain not only to see my daughter but also as a sort of pilgrimage to search for God and ask Him what He wanted me to do next, since everything I had tried seemed to inevitably lead to failure. I needed God's help to re-evaluate my life in order to carry on and be at peace with my spirit. And there He was, larger than life itself, not able to be seen, yet I knew He was there, just as I had known Jesus had come down to be with me in my tiny apartment on the beach almost twenty years earlier. It was as if He was telling me *"I Am here. Ask anything you want."* And I tell you, I felt about the size of a pine cone in a national forest as I stood there on that mountaintop wondering what to say to my Creator. And I know the lyrics in most country songs tell how the singer always kneels down on his or her knees and prays, but I just stood there, looked up to Heaven and said,

"God will you please direct my paths? I am tired of searching for things that never work out. Please just let me do your will, God. Amen." And that was it. About thirty seconds later the rumbling sound faded away and I was left with a memory and a story to tell for the rest of my life.

> *The voice of the Lord is over the waters;*
>   *the God of glory thunders,*
>   *the Lord thunders over the mighty waters.*
> *The voice of the Lord is powerful;*

the voice of the Lord is majestic.

Psalm 29:3-4 (NIV)

And I do consider myself luckier than most; after all, I have had the honor and amazing blessings of being visited by both God and Jesus in my lifetime, and I don't take that lightly. I know I had to wait thirty years for the first visitation and another twenty years for the second; and that's not even to mention the times when I didn't feel their presence but they let me know they were there. I know you're waiting to find out if He answered my prayer or if the whole episode turned out to be my imagination and wishful thinking getting the best of me. Well, let me tell you the rest of the story and you can figure it out for yourself.

I left North Carolina for home first thing the next morning. My wife was happy to see me and I told her all about the trip, including the part about talking to God. She sounded a little skeptical but said it was great that my daughter and I got to spend some time together. I continued to do volunteer work for the museum and the Red Cross, and then a couple weeks later my wife told me that while I was out a guy had called from a hospital to talk to me about a job. Long story short, I called him back, got hired to work at a hospital in the next town, we left Orlando, and my wife found the house of our dreams two miles away from my new job. I could stop right here and just say, *'and we lived happily ever after'* but I've just got to let everyone know what God did for us since our talk up on the mountain.

Every good and perfect gift comes from above, coming down from the Father of the Heavenly lights, who does not change like shifting shadows.

James 1:17 (NIV)

The first thing I did after we got settled into our new home was search for all the hiking and biking trails in the area. There were so many to choose from that were listed online, and I believe I hiked or biked just about every one of them during that first year. Kelly hiked a select few with me during the cooler winter and spring months, as she has never tolerated the heat of summers in Florida. Along the way I even discovered a new passion in kayaking, a hobby I had never before been interested in. It's a wonderful sport and pastime and deserves a try by anyone who enjoys being around nature and/or water. For about a year during 2009/2010 I was crazy about kayaking the rivers of Central Florida and regularly went paddling on the weekends, whether on the Wekiva, the Econlockhatchee, or the Blackwater Creek, while still managing to play hockey during the week. My wife also enjoyed the serenity of paddling the calm waters of the Wekiva River, so we bought a tandem kayak and learned how to paddle in unison. Boy was that interesting. If you've never gone kayaking or canoeing with your spouse, it's something you need to try; quite an accomplishment when you finally get it right. Less patient couples should be aware that learning to paddle in unison isn't as easy as you might think, and could lead to, at the very least an argumentative first time out and, at the very worst an unexpected dunk in the drink. For more on our exploits into kayaking, my book **"Biking and Kayaking Through Tribal Florida"** (2018), is available on Amazon.com in both black & white and color editions. Why the strange title? It's actually quite simple. Not wanting to write just another book on the joys of kayaking or where to paddle in Florida, I added a slight twist to the subject. The title itself is a pretty good clue as to what the book is about, so why not let your curiosity get the best of you and just read it? The book also indicates how I eventually lost interest in kayaking and sold both of them within a year after our maiden voyage down the Wekiva River in a rental kayak from Wekiva Springs State Park. It had something to do with a large gator in the Econ, but that wasn't the only reason. I was getting more involved in hockey and wanted to learn the goalie position, so I purchased all the necessary gear, simply known as 'The Pads.' Paradoxically, the more I got into hockey the more I got into running races. I began placing or winning my age group in every race I entered; hard not to stay focused on racing when you are placing well and winning. By the end of 2009 I had already quit one hockey team and was barely scoring three goals a season on another. I wanted to try my luck at goaltending but it's a tough position to learn, especially at the youthful age of 51. So I kept putting it off and only tried playing in goal at a handful of skate 'n shoot practices, where a few kids would shoot on me because no other goalies wanted to take shots from kids. Ever since I started playing goal, my motto has been to take shots from anyone, anytime, anywhere. I figured I would have to think that way to excel in the position. By the end of 2010 I felt I was ready to play between the pipes. But as difficult a position goaltending was to learn, it was even harder trying to find a team that would let a brand new goalie play for them. No hockey team likes to lose. It's the same in all sports, I know. But hockey players hate to lose. I guess it's just the nature of the game. Anyway, at the end of the fall 2010 season, the rink management decided to start up a new rookie league for beginning players. I thought that would be a great opportunity. Then during the final game of the season I got poked in the eye with the butt end of an opponent's stick, and that sealed the deal. Asked my brother if he thought I should keep playing and risk another eye injury, of which I'd had several in my life by then, and he asked if I'd ever considered playing goal. Well that was all it took. I told him I'd already been practicing the position a little and was thinking about playing goalie in the new league starting up. With my brother's blessings I did just that. To say I had better luck as a goaltender than I ever had as a forward or defenseman is to admit the facts. My first season in goal my team won the championship game at the end of the season, and we repeated the following season. In the summer of 2011 I got drafted to another team, our arch rivals from the previous two seasons. We lost my first game as a goalie and then went undefeated for most of the season, winning nine games in a row and easily leading the league all season long. But then came the championship game for the winner's cup, and the other team wanted it bad. We jumped out front and looked unbeatable after the first two periods. I was stopping everything they tried their best to get by me, and we looked like sure winners. I began thinking about the fact that this would be my third championship in three tries, and I think my team was already drinking beer out of the winner's cup as well. But, what's that old saying? It ain't over till it's over? And in hockey that means until that final buzzer goes off with a definite winner. Our game went down to the wire. The other team scored four unanswered goals in the third period, forcing a goalie shootout. The other goalie, a seasoned amateur from Canada (I forgot which part), played the second half of the game flawlessly, letting nothing go by. On the other hand, I let four goals in during the last period of the game. We were both on a roll and the writing was on the wall. It was a nail-biter for sure and we both let in the first two shots in the shootout. My dream of three straight championships ended when the other goalie stopped the fourth shot and I let one go by. The traditional bench clearing celebration would be for the other team for the first time in three seasons. How could I be disappointed? My teammates however had definitely been caught by surprise. There are few things as depressing in sports as losing a game when it was an almost sure bet.

After three magically successful seasons living out one of my childhood fantasies, I decided not to sign up for the next season, figuring there was nowhere to go from there but down. But I still enjoyed playing in goal, so throughout the remainder of 2011 I continued to mind the net for the kids at the afternoon skate 'n shoots, filled in for another goalie who played in an old-timers league on Saturday mornings, and also played in Sunday afternoon clinics that preceded the Sunday night league games, featuring the best players at the rink. I just didn't play in a league. Sometimes after Sunday clinics I would stay over and watch my favorite elite league team, the Can-Ams, play their Sunday night game. Mind you I was playing goalie three to four times a week, which was quite a lot for someone not even playing in a league. Goalies require a lot of practice time to keep their edge if they want to maintain a decent save percentage. One Sunday afternoon following a clinic something really cool happened. Two other goalies and I were in the locker room changing into our street clothes when in walks Peter, the captain of the Can-Ams. Pete sometimes participated in clinics, practices, and other rink functions so we figured he was just passing through. But then he sat down on the bench. What was going on?

"Any of you want to play goalie for us?"

He looked around the room. I looked at the other two guys. We were all in our forties or fifties and had just spent the past 45 minutes taking continuous shots on goal. But I was curious, and the other two didn't look interested.

"You mean in a game? For the Can-Ams?" I said.

"In a game," he replied.

Then it was just a matter of getting the words out of my mouth fast enough so the other guys wouldn't have a chance.

"Heck yeah!"

And that's the story of how I got to play goalie for my favorite elite league team. Now the elite league by definition was made up of players with either college experience, semi-pro, professional, or all of the above. And I can tell you there was at least one guy playing on the opposing team that day who was playing pro hockey in the ECHL during the winter season and skating at our local rink all summer. So these guys could shoot and score. I had never had to face so many quality shots during a game in my life. I did okay for my first time in the upper league. The regular goalie showed up right before the third period, so I let him finish the game, thinking he might be able to salvage something from a 4-goal deficit and possibly even win the game. He was, after all, one of the best goalies in that league at the time. But we lost anyway and I figured *wow,* what an experience, and that would probably never happen again anyway. After the game I stepped back onto the ice and shook hands with all the players during the traditional post-game handshake. It was indescribable to be out there participating with the very players I had looked up to in awe as I watched them play their Sunday games. In return I got a little more respect after that milestone day, but they probably still considered me a slug because I hadn't finished the game and opted to let the other goalie finish. So in their eyes I still hadn't played an entire game in the elite league. With the chances of getting another shot at it anytime soon slim to none, I quickly got back into the old routine of practicing three or four days a week.

The following year, 2012 more or less stayed on cruise control; more foot races and more hockey. The best news that year was that my wife Kelly passed her 5-year mark of being cancer free. After five years the medical community considered a patient cancer free and no longer required regular checkups. What a relief that was! She could live a normal life without worrying about the cancer coming back. God be praised!

And the prayer offered in faith will make the sick person well; the Lord will raise them up. If they have sinned they will be forgiven.

Therefore confess your sins to each other and pray for each other so that you may be healed.

The prayer of a righteous person is powerful and effective.   James 5:15-17 (NIV)

By the end of the year it was time to try something new, so I scaled back on hockey and running and decided to go back to school. In the spring of 2013 I was enrolled in a masters program toward a degree in exercise science, a subject both my wife and I figured would be right up my alley. I didn't even make it past the first semester. I'd never seen such technical terminology and scientific methodology applied to exercise in my entire life. I got an **A** on my research paper on geriatric aging with vs. without exercise, but almost flunked both the mid-term and final exams. So much for that idea. With me and my goal-oriented psyche, the question is always what to do next. It was time to re-evaluate once again, but this time I wouldn't have the benefit of walking right up to God's doorstep and asking Him what to do. How does one reach

God when there are no mountains around to climb? The only answer can be prayer, in one's quiet place. My quiet place had been a favorite trail in the woods where I would often jog or walk to clear out my head and give my thoughts to God. With no other goals to set in the hockey world, I decided to start ramping up my running program. When my sister came up for a visit that fall, she asked if I'd ever considered running long distance races. That lit a new spark in my soul and I began training for half marathons, and ran my first one in Orlando. I finished in under two hours and was hooked, then signed up for three more in the spring of 2014. My wife and I drove up to Pensacola in the pouring rain in March and then all the way to Kitty Hawk, North Carolina for what turned out to be my last half marathon, in April. My right heel began aching toward the end of the last race and since the pain didn't go away, I decided to cease all running throughout the summer months. The following fall running season however, I returned to the 5K races, figuring they would do less damage to my heel. All they really did was prolong the inevitable. I won more races but again, the writing was on the wall and by the spring of 2016 I had run my last race, maybe for the rest of my life. The pain just would not let up as long as I was running. I never thought my goalie career would outlast my running career, but only God knows what is in store for our future.

There was nothing much left on my bucket list so I just bought a mountain bike and started doing some trail riding; that didn't seem to bother my foot much at all. I had visions of someday entering mountain bike races in Florida and North Georgia, but as I edged closer to the big 6-0, competition didn't have the same attraction it once had on my heart and soul. Just having fun doing whatever I was doing became more important.

On a side note, another ancient hobby I rekindled in the twilight of my fifties was playing the trumpet, the instrument I had played in the high school band. In December of 2014 an orchestra from the Orlando community arts played their annual Christmas concert in one of the large stadium-sized churches close to us, and Kelly and I decided to go. They sounded really professional and put on a good show. As I listened I couldn't help but wonder what it would be like to play in a large band again after all those years. When we got home I went online to see if I could find out the qualifications for playing in their orchestra. There didn't seem to be any, except for owning an instrument and being willing to show up for practices on Sunday nights, so I applied. Next thing you know I'm up on stage playing in an orchestra, which seemed to grow exponentially with each concert we played over the next two years. What an experience getting to play with all of those fine musicians who made me feel right at home from the very beginning. Turns out that performing in their Christmas concert one year after my wife and I had watched them from the balcony would be my favorite concert out of the six or seven I participated in. The violins, brass, woodwinds, percussion, and the singers in the huge chorus all helped make it a very special Christmas for me. I'm sure we did the same for the audience who attended. I miss it sometimes and it is something I would consider doing all over again after I retire from the hospital.

For my 60th birthday all I really wanted was to start playing hockey again, so I got back into playing goalie in the Sunday afternoon clinics. There were a handful of old familiar faces who played every week, but mostly new guys just learning the game. It was pretty fun but by my 61st birthday I was ready for a new challenge so I decided, after eight years off, to get back into a league. It was really cool to play with referees officiating once again; they make a game feel so much more 'official.' Once again I played for a winning team and we took almost every game that season. Yet there was something else about that first comeback season that I will never forget. Perhaps lightning never strikes twice in the same place (something my brother used to say), but maybe after eight years go by it can strike again. When you read this next story you might come to the same conclusion.

We were pretty deep into the season, my first full season in eight years, and were up 3-2 with less than ten minutes remaining in the game. I had been having a good game, allowing less than one goal per period, pretty good for me. I've never been a shutout goaltender; I just know what it takes to win hockey games. Sometimes you just know when your team is going to win, and I was certain we would win that one. With only five minutes left in the game, the referee blew the whistle for no apparent reason. That was weird enough, and I kept asking any teammate skating by what the whistle was for. No one seemed to know. Then the loud buzzer went off that usually signals the end of the period or game. Now all the players were wondering what was going on. Again no one seemed to know. Had the scorekeeper hit the buzzer by mistake? Were they ending the game prematurely because they were running behind schedule? The referee skated over to the scorekeeper's booth to find out what was going on, so at least we would all know soon enough. After chatting at the booth for a minute or so, the ref skated straight over to me, which I thought was pretty odd. I asked him what was up.

"You wanna play in the next game?" he asked.

"Which league?" I asked.

"Advanced."

I had thought so but just wanted to confirm.

"What team?" I asked.

"CanAms," was the reply.

"Heck yeah!" I said.

Now I know you may have just read about the same thing happening to me just a few pages back in this book. But the truth is it was just about the same situation with the same two teams eight years apart. I was blown away before the game had even started. I wanted so badly to improve on my previous performance, but I was 61 years old for crying out loud, and these guys were some of the best hockey players in Central Florida. I had a couple of things going for me, and they were both the caliber of at least two of the players on my team. One was a former ECHL player who had played on the opposing team in the previous game eight years earlier. The other was an AHL prospect who had also played in the previous game, but for the Can Ams. In addition we would have the only other player who had been with the Can Ams for at least ten years, one of the best defensemen in the league. All the other players, except for the captain Pete, had joined the team since the last time I played for them. We had a chance. When I passed through the dressing room before the game, the AHL prospect and the veteran defenseman were still in there.

"I guess I'm going to be your goalie," I said, trying to be as confident as possible for someone who had only played in one previous Advanced League game, eight years earlier. They both recognized me right away as the guy who always watched their Sunday evening games.

"Hey, good luck out there goalie," said David, the AHL prospect, who had been averaging about 5 points per game that season.

"Thanks man," I said as we shook hands. And then under my breath I continued, "and this time we're going to finish the game."

I wasn't sure if they would understand what I was talking about so I didn't say it very loud, and didn't repeat it. But if there was one thing I knew for sure about this game, it was this: Whether we were winning or losing after the second period, and no matter what the score, I wasn't coming off that ice until the game was over. I had waited eight years for another opportunity like this one, and there was no way I was going to leave any 'if onlys' on that ice. I might never get another chance ever again. By that point in my career I had been playing it week by week, never knowing when my last game might be.

So the same referee who had worked the game right before the advanced league game, the one who had asked if I wanted to play, would be our ref for the Can Ams vs. Lyons game. Once we all took our places for the opening faceoff he skated over to me and asked if I was ready.

"Ready as I'll ever be," I said. "I figured you would be playing on our team," I said, half jokingly. He sometimes played for the Lyons.

"I wish," he said, and then skated over to center ice to drop the puck. I wished too. That guy was about the fastest and highest scoring player at the rink that year, and as this book goes to print he has recently signed a contract to play in the AHL. The only 'if' I know for sure is if he were on our team in addition to the players we had, we would have won. That I am quite sure of.

As soon as the puck dropped we all put on our game faces and started playing some hockey. The play was fast and furious but I had watched these guys play against each other and against other teams time and time again, and I knew exactly what they were capable of. The only surprise I met through the first twenty minutes of the game was that we were winning 4-2 after the first period. I tried my best not to let it go to my head but I did recall that the score in the previous game when we met eight years earlier had been the same after one period, only reversed. I had allowed only two goals in the first period, in the Advanced League, at the age of 61. It was very hard not to jump up and down ecstatically just knowing all this. The perks to playing well for these guys were that every now and then, whenever they got the opportunity, like after a whistle, or after the puck was cleared down the ice, one of them would skate by, tap my pads with his stick, and say stuff like, 'You're doing great, keep it up,' or 'Nice save, goalie.'

One of my favorites was during the second period, after I let a goal whiz by and got a little upset about it, Mike the ECHL player skated over to me, all out of breath and sweating like he had been giving it his all, and said,

"Don't get frustrated. These guys are going to be taking a lot of shots. You're doin' good." Then he tapped my pads and skated over to his faceoff position. That was awesome. Stuff like that made it all worthwhile.

By the end of the second period the game started going a little more like I thought it would. My stellar performance in the first period could not be equaled in the second, and the score after two periods of play was 7-7. We were still in the hunt but the Lyons had always been a third period team; you know the kind of team that tests their opponents in the first and second periods to find out their weaknesses and then pounces on them in the third period.

Before the last period began, David skated down to my net and asked if I was having fun. My eyes got really big and I smiled like a little kid and said,

"Man, this is freakin' awesome!" Then I had to comment on the game he was having, nothing short of remarkable. "How many goals have you scored, four or five?"

"I don't know, seven?" he said, indicating that he hadn't been keeping track, just scoring as many goals as he could. Both teams had been playing with light benches; the Lyons had seven players and we had only six (plus the two goalies). They were going to forfeit the game at the start when the Can Ams goalie didn't show up; then they found me and pretty much knew I wouldn't say no. The Lyons had given up a key player in Mike to the Can Ams just so they could play the game. And it turned out to be a pretty fair game, really. Mike and David scored all but one of our goals I think. We went goal for goal with them all the way to the 15:00 minute mark in the game. With only 5:00 minutes remaining and both teams exhausted, the scoreboard read 9-9. Mike skated down to my net holding his stomach and doubled over like he was going to be sick. I thought oh no, that's not good, but I didn't think we were in trouble, I mean there were only five minutes left in the game. All through the game I had been praying to God that He would just get me through the game and give us a respectable score. That's all, just finish respectably. I thought 9-9 with five minutes left in the game was pretty respectable, so I knew God had been listening and watching over us throughout the game. Then Mike left the ice. Pete, the Can Ams captain (Remember him from the first game in 2011?) called a timeout and we all skated to the bench.

The big question would be, 'Now what do we do?' We were all exhausted, Mike had left the game and we had no substitutes on the bench. Pete had the option of forfeiting the game to the Lyons, but like a true hockey player he said,

"Let's just play."

So we did; finished out the game, but my guys were toast. I didn't get much help for the next five minutes and it was just like I said, the Lyons pounced on us, scoring five goals in the last five minutes of the game.

When I look back on that game I sometimes feel disappointed, sure. It would have been a minor miracle to have finished the game with a one or two goal deficit instead of six; a major miracle to have actually won, even though we came very close and would have been right there in the game until the final buzzer if Mike had not cramped up. Part of me will probably always feel like I was cheated out of a decent score; but that would be the fool in me. In reality I didn't even belong in that game. Truth is I have never belonged in an elite or advanced league game. College level, semi-pro, and pro level are the only players allowed in that league, and it is only by the grace of God and the good-hearted nature of a select group of players in the advanced league that I have been allowed and privileged to play in two games. But I did finish the second one, and no one will ever take that away from me, especially now that it is in print. Would I play for the Can Ams if ever asked again? What do you think? I was in fact hopeful they would ask me again the following season or the season after that, but as this book goes to print, none of us have so much as ice skated in over two months because of COVID-19. All rinks have been closed and we have no idea when they will reopen or what the 'new normal' will look like for ice hockey. Not only that but I just turned 62 and haven't skated in three months. Playing goalie requires a lot of effort, preparation, desire, practice, and gumption. In short, if my body, heart, and mind are not all in when the rink reopens and hockey restarts, I may never play in a league again.

And that pretty much brings us up to the current situation; social distancing is the new catch phrase for 2020. How long it will last is anybody's guess. Some important people in the know are saying things may never get back to the way they were before COVID-19. If that is the case our future has just turned another page. But I don't want the end of this book to be all about how COVID-19 changed the world. It didn't. And only our response to it can change our lives entirely. We are all still going to leave this Earth one day. That has always been the case. The most important thing to know is if you are ready. You will know if you are ready; it's a state of mind. There are only two ways to be ready; one as a Christian and one as a non-Christian. If you are ready as a non-Christian you may just not care if you die. You accepted your fate in your youth and know that no one on Earth has ever promised you weren't going to die one day. And you're okay with that. And I'm okay with you being like that. No one can tell you how to live your life, how to think or what to believe. But like it says on a large wooden plaque over a doorway in our home,

As for me and my house, we will serve the LORD."

Joshua 24:15 (KJV)

I like the concept of my soul living on after my body has died. Also I love the fact that the Bible says all we have to do is pick up our cross (no small feat) and follow

Jesus, and we can have eternal life in Jesus Christ. And I would much rather finish this chapter, the longest and most important one in the book, discussing eternal life with our Lord and Savior than discussing a pandemic that God Himself will destroy if we all would just humble ourselves and proclaim Jesus Christ as our Lord. Can I get an Amen?

12 EXERCISE IS OF SOME VALUE/ EPILOGUE

The exercise bug hit me at around the age of 16, and 45 years later, in spite of aching joints, slower metabolism, and all those other hindrances that go along with growing old, I still manage to dedicate about ten hours a week to different forms of exercise that will hopefully keep me in decent health for my retirement years. Ten hours a week doesn't sound like enough time to make much of a difference but it is said that it is the *intensity* of the exercise that counts rather than the amount. We all know, or at least know *of* people whose lives revolve around exercise for one reason or another. Some are paid athletes, and for them exercise and strength building are essential elements of their training regimen. Others are what are sometimes referred to as "weekend athletes". They work full time jobs during the week and compete in some type of sport on the weekends. Like me they try to get in as much training during the week as possible, time permitting. Some of us take our training more seriously than others, perhaps putting in as much as twenty or even thirty hours of extracurricular activities during the week, in spite of working full-time jobs. This behavior often leads those who do little to no training to judge these overachievers as being overly vain. They figure that the only reason for exercising that much is because some workout zealots care about nothing or nobody except themselves. There are bound to be as many opinions on this subject as there are personality types, and it wouldn't do any good to list them all here. But those of us who have been accused of exercising excessively at times, perhaps for an important competition, series of competitions, or maybe even a competitive season sometimes wonder if there is any truth to the naysayers' claims that exercise is pure vanity. And so we must seek the answer from the only source that is 100% reliable and truthful, the Holy Bible. What's that, you say? Exercise is in the Bible? No way! Yes it is, and though there are no specifics as to how much or what kind of exercise is recommended for the Christian who wants to workout in a way that pleases God, Paul the Apostle often referred to running races as a metaphor pertaining to the endurance and discipline needed to live a righteous yet simple life.

Do you not know that in a race all the runners run, but only one gets the prize? Run in such a way as to get the prize. Everyone who competes in the games goes into strict training. They do it to get a crown that will not last, but we do it to get a crown that will last forever. Therefore I do not run like someone running aimlessly. I do not fight like a boxer beating the air. No, I strike a blow to my body and make it my slave so that after I have preached to others, I myself will not be disqualified for the prize. 1 Corinthians 9:24-27 (NIV)

Have nothing to do with godless myths and old wives' tales; rather, train yourself to be godly. For physical training is of some value, but godliness has value for all things, holding promise for both the present life and the life to come. This is a trustworthy saying that deserves full acceptance. That is why we labor and strive, because we have put our hope in the living God, who is the Savior of all people, and especially of those who believe. 1 Timothy 4:7-10 (NIV)

So what do we make of the writings of Paul the Apostle, who obviously felt that the virtues required for winning at races and other competitions were similar to the virtues needed to 'fight the good fight', as he would write to Timothy in the same letter two chapters later. I'm not a Bible interpreter, any more than the average church goer or Scripture follower. Nor do I see it as my place to make public lengthy commentary on Bible Scripture; that should be reserved for ordained ministers of the cloth and scholars with at least a master's degree in theology. I just wanted to put it out there that godly people, such as the people Paul commonly referred to in his letters in the New Testament, have been running races and competing in sports since Biblical times. Use that information for whatever it is worth to you.

I am extremely grateful for Paul's inclusion of running and competitive sports in his writings, even if he used them mostly as metaphors. It shows he appreciated the time and effort athletes put into their chosen pastime/sport. Should we as athletes feel a little more justified or vindicated knowing that our passions and pursuits have been given the approval of Paul the Apostle, among other major Christian characters in the Bible? Even the prophet Isaiah wrote about endurance in the Old Testament:

Even youths grow tired and weary,
    and young men stumble and fall;
   but those who hope in the Lord
    will renew their strength.

They will soar on wings like eagles;

they will run and not grow weary,

they will walk and not grow faint.

Isaiah 40:30-31 (NIV)

One of my favorites. I wore a jersey during a half marathon in Pensacola that bore this inscription on the back along with the image of an eagle in flight. Reciting this verse during the last couple of miles literally got me through the race without quitting.

My take from all this plus the fact that I've spent all of my adult life trying to maintain some type of exercise regime, whether it be mowing grass, working out, riding bikes, surfing, running, or playing hockey, is that humans were created to be spiritual beings first and foremost, but we were also designed for some type of exercise. The anatomy and physiology of our bodies proves that. The more we exercise, to a point, the better we feel and the healthier we are. And I think that as long as we don't become obsessed over it and put it above everything and everybody else in our lives, we should just go on exercising to our heart's content. So find a form of exercise you enjoy and give thanks to God that you have the ability and desire to keep doing it. He will smile down on you and your joyful soul and I'd bet Paul the Apostle will be up in Heaven with a proud grin on his face, knowing that you will 'finish the race.'

Made in the USA
San Bernardino, CA
07 June 2020